irresistible cakes

irresistible cakes

a celebration of fabulous bakes for all occasions

sarah maxwell and angela nilsen

This edition is published by Hermes House

Hermes House is an imprint of Anness Publishing Ltd
Hermes House, 88–89 Blackfriars Road, London SE1 8HA
tel. 020 7401 2077; fax 020 7633 9499; info@anness.com

Published in the USA by Hermes House, Anness Publishing Inc.
27 West 20th Street, New York, NY 10011; fax 212 807 6813

A CIP catalogue record for this book is available from the British Library.

Publisher: Joanna Lorenz
Project Editors: Judith Simons and Clare Nicholson
Photographer: Tim Hill
Home Economists: Sarah Maxwell and Angela Nilsen
Assisted by Teresa Goldfinch
Stylist: Sarah Maxwell
Design: Axis Design Editions Ltd

1 3 5 7 9 10 8 6 4 2

For all recipes, quantities are given in both metric and imperial measures and, where appropriate, measures are also given in standard cups and spoons. Follow one set, but not a mixture, because they are not interchangeable.

Standard spoon and cup measures are level.
1 tsp = 5ml, 1 tbsp = 15ml, 1 cup = 250ml/8fl oz

Australian standard tablespoons are 20ml. Australian readers should use 3 tsp in place of 1 tbsp for measuring small quantities of gelatine, cornflour, salt, etc.

Medium eggs are used unless otherwise stated.

Contents

Introduction

The fabulous cakes in this book are divided into three, equally imaginative, sections. The first contains a fine selection of classic cakes, ranging from the German Battenberg to a traditional rich chocolate creation. This is followed by a chapter devoted to really beautiful cakes, each for a special occasion such as New Year, St Valentine's Day or a birthday. Then comes the children's party cakes – truly creative, they include a clown and a magic carpet complete with the genie of the lamp.

Finally, many of these recipes feature standard cake mixes, such as quick-mix sponge and rich fruit cake, and icings, such as marzipan and sugarpaste. Where this is the case, the mix or icing appears at the end of the book in the chapter on basic cakes and basic icings. This section tells you exactly how to make each cake and quantities are given for all the shapes and sizes included in the recipes in this book.

Within each recipe all the ingredients are given in metric, imperial and cup measurements. When following a recipe, always work with one set of ingredients only as mixing them might result in disappointment. For the best results, use eggs which are at room temperature, and sift flour after you have measured it. If you sift the flour from a fair height, it will have more chance to aerate and lighten.

No two ovens are alike. Buy a reliable oven thermometer and test the temperature of your oven. When possible, bake in the centre of the oven where the heat is more likely to be constant. If using a fan assisted oven, follow the manufacturer's guidelines for baking. Good quality cake tins can also improve your results, as they conduct heat more efficiently.

Whatever the occasion, whatever the cake, this book will guarantee you cakes which not only look good – they taste great too.

Classic Cakes

Classic Cakes includes traditional favourites, perfect for teas, picnics, and formal and informal gatherings. Battenberg, Shortcake, Dundee cake, Roulade, Chocolate gâteau, Madeira cake and many more are included, sometimes in their classic form and sometimes excitingly reinterpreted for this book.

Crunchy-topped Madeira Cake

Traditionally served with a glass of Madeira wine in Victorian England, this light sponge still makes a perfect tea-time treat.

INGREDIENTS

Serves 8–10

200 g/7 oz/14 tbsp butter, softened
finely grated zest of 1 lemon
150 g/5 oz/¾ cup caster sugar
3 size 3 eggs
75 g/3 oz/¾ cup plain flour, sifted
150 g/5 oz/1¼ cups self-raising flour, sifted

For the Topping

3 tbsp clear honey
115 g/4 oz/¾ cup plus 2 tbsp chopped mixed peel
50 g/2 oz/½ cup flaked almonds

STORING

This cake can be kept for up to three days in an airtight container.

1 Preheat the oven to 180°C/350°F/Gas 4. Grease a 450 g/1 lb loaf tin, line the base and sides with greaseproof paper and grease the paper.

2 ▲ Place the butter, lemon zest and sugar in a mixing bowl and beat until light and fluffy. Beat in the eggs, one at a time, until evenly blended.

3 ▲ Sift together the flours, then stir into the egg mixture. Transfer the cake mixture to the prepared tin and smooth the surface.

4 ▲ Bake in the centre of the oven for 45–50 minutes or until a skewer inserted into the centre of the cake comes out clean. Leave the cake in the tin for about 5 minutes. Turn out on to a wire rack, peel off the lining paper and leave to cool completely.

5 ▲ To make the topping, place the honey, chopped mixed peel and almonds in a small saucepan and heat gently until the honey melts. Remove from the heat and stir briefly to coat the peel and almonds, then spread over the top of the cake. Allow to cool completely before serving.

Gorgeous Chocolate Cake

This recipe will definitely make you famous. Make sure you serve it with paper and pens, as everyone will want to take down the recipe.

INGREDIENTS

Serves 8–10

175 g/6 oz/¾ cup butter, softened
115 g/4 oz/½ cup caster sugar
250 g/9 oz/9 squares plain chocolate, melted
200 g/7 oz/2⅓ cups ground almonds
4 size 3 eggs, separated
115 g/4 oz/4 squares white chocolate, melted, to decorate

STORING

This cake can be kept for up to four days in an airtight container.

1 Preheat the oven to 180°C/350°F/Gas 4. Grease a deep 21 cm/8½ inch springform cake tin, then line the base with greaseproof paper and grease the paper.

2 ▲ Place 115 g/4 oz/½ cup of the butter and all the sugar in a mixing bowl and beat until light and fluffy. Add two thirds of the plain chocolate, the ground almonds and the egg yolks and beat until evenly blended.

3 ▲ Whisk the egg whites in another clean, dry bowl until stiff. Fold them into the chocolate mixture, then transfer to the prepared tin and smooth the surface. Bake for 50–55 minutes or until a skewer inserted into the centre of the cake comes out clean. Leave the cake in the tin for about 5 minutes, then turn out on to a wire rack, peel off the lining paper and leave to cool completely.

4 ▲ Place the remaining butter and remaining melted plain chocolate in a saucepan. Heat very gently, stirring constantly, until melted. Pour over the cake, allowing the topping to coat the sides too. Leave to set for at least an hour. To decorate, fill a piping bag with the melted white chocolate and snip the end. Drizzle all around the edges to make a double border. Use any remaining chocolate to make leaves (see Trailing Orchid Wedding cake, steps 2 and 3).

Tip

Place a large sheet of greaseproof paper or a baking sheet under the wire rack before pouring the chocolate topping over the cake. This will catch all the drips and keep the work surface clean.

utumn Passionettes

Perfect for a tea party or packed lunch, this passion cake mixture can also be made as one big cake to serve for a celebration or as a dessert.

INGREDIENTS
Makes 24
150 g/5 oz/3/4 cup butter, melted
200 g/7 oz/7/8 cup soft light brown sugar
115 g/4 oz/1 cup carrots, peeled and finely grated
50 g/2 oz/1 cup dessert apples, peeled and finely grated
pinch of salt
1–2 tsp ground mixed spice
2 size 3 eggs
200 g/7 oz/1 3/4 cups self-raising flour
2 tsp baking powder
115 g/4 oz/1 cup shelled walnuts, finely chopped

For the Topping
175 g/6 oz/3/4 cup full-fat soft cheese
4–5 tbsp single cream
50 g/2 oz/1/2 cup icing sugar, sifted
25 g/1 oz/1/4 cup shelled walnuts, halved
2 tsp cocoa powder, sifted

STORING
Both the large and small cakes can be kept for up to four days in an airtight container.

1 Preheat the oven to 180°C/350°F/ Gas 4. Arrange 24 fairy cake paper cases in bun tins and put to one side.

2 ▲ Place the butter, sugar, carrots, apples, salt, mixed spice and eggs in a mixing bowl and beat well to combine.

3 ▲ Sift together the flour and baking powder into a small bowl, then sift again into the mixing bowl. Add the chopped walnuts and fold in until evenly blended.

4 ▲ Fill the paper cases half-full with the cake mixture, then bake for 20–25 minutes, or until a skewer inserted into the centres of the cakes comes out clean.

5 Leave the cakes in the tins for about 5 minutes, before transferring them to a wire rack to cool completely.

6 ▲ To make the topping, place the full-fat soft cheese in a mixing bowl and beat in the cream and icing sugar until smooth. Put a dollop of the topping in the centre of each cake, then decorate with the walnuts. Dust with sifted cocoa powder and allow the icing to set before serving.

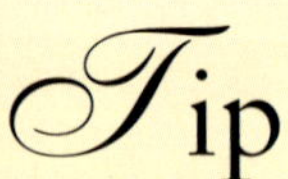

ip

To make one big cake, which will serve 6–8, grease a 20 cm/8 inch fluted American bundt cake tin and line the base with greaseproof paper. Grease the paper. Place all of the cake mixture in the tin and bake for about 1 1/4 hours, or until a skewer inserted into the centre of the cake comes out clean. Leave the cake in the tin for about 5 minutes. Turn out on to a wire rack, peel off the lining paper and leave to cool completely. Decorate with the topping mixture, walnuts and sifted cocoa powder.

Chestnut Cake

An Italian speciality, this is definitely a cake to mark an occasion. Rich, moist and heavy, it can be made up to a week in advance and kept, undecorated, wrapped and stored in an airtight container. Allow the cake to come to room temperature before serving.

INGREDIENTS
Serves 8–10
150 g/5 oz/1¼ cups plain flour
pinch of salt
225 g/8 oz/1 cup butter, softened
150 g/5 oz/¾ cup caster sugar
439 g/15½ oz can chestnut purée
9 size 3 eggs, separated
7 tbsp dark rum
300 ml/½ pint/1¼ cups double cream

To Decorate
marrons glacés, chopped
icing sugar, sifted

STORING
Once decorated do not store.

1 Preheat the oven to 180°C/350°F/Gas 4. Grease a 21 cm/8½ inch springform cake tin, line the base with greaseproof paper and grease the paper.

2 Sift together the flour and salt, and set aside. Place the butter and three-quarters of the sugar in a bowl and beat until fluffy.

3 ▲ Fold in two-thirds of the chestnut purée, alternating with the egg yolks, and beat. Fold in the flour and salt.

4 ▲ Whisk the egg whites in a clean, dry bowl until stiff. Beat a little of the egg whites into the chestnut mixture, until evenly blended, then fold in the remainder.

5 ▲ Transfer the cake mixture to the prepared tin and smooth the surface. Bake in the centre of the oven for about 1¼ hours, or until a skewer inserted into the centre of the cake comes out clean.

6 Place the cake, still in the tin, on a wire rack. Using a skewer, pierce holes evenly all over the cake. Sprinkle 4 tbsp of the rum over the top, then allow the cake to cool completely.

7 ▲ Remove the cake from the tin, peel off the lining paper and cut horizontally into two layers. Place the bottom layer on a serving plate. Whisk the cream in a mixing bowl with the remaining rum, sugar and chestnut purée until thick and smooth.

8 To assemble the cake, spread two-thirds of the chestnut cream mixture over the bottom layer and place the other layer on top. Spread some of the remaining chestnut cream over the top and sides of the cake, then fill a greaseproof paper piping bag, fitted with a star nozzle, with the rest of the chestnut mixture. Pipe big swirls around the outside edge of the cake. Decorate with the marrons glacés and sifted icing sugar.

Tip

In order to have the most control over a piping bag, it is important to hold it in a relaxed position. You may find it easier to hold it with one or both hands.

Mocha-hazelnut Battenberg

The traditional Battenberg cake originated in Germany when the Prince of Battenberg married Queen Victoria's daughter, Beatrice. This recipe is a variation of the original theme.

Ingredients

Serves 6–8

115 g/4 oz/½ cup butter, softened
115 g/4 oz/½ cup caster sugar
2 size 3 eggs
115 g/4 oz/1 cup self-raising flour, sifted
50 g/2 oz/⅔ cup ground hazelnuts
2 tsp coffee essence
1 tbsp cocoa powder

To Finish

7 tbsp apricot jam, warmed and sieved
225 g/8 oz yellow marzipan
50 g/2 oz/⅔ cup ground hazelnuts
sifted icing sugar, for rolling out
ground hazelnuts, to decorate

STORING

This cake can be kept for up to three days in an airtight container.

1 Preheat the oven to 180°C/350°F/ Gas 4. Grease an 18 cm/7 inch square cake tin, line the base with greaseproof paper and grease the paper.

2 ▲ Place the butter and sugar in a bowl and beat until fluffy. Gradually beat in the eggs, then fold in the flour. Transfer half the mixture to another bowl.

3 ▲ Stir the ground hazelnuts into one half of the cake mixture and the coffee essence and cocoa powder into the other half.

4 ▲ Prepare a strip of foil to fit the width and height of the cake tin, then place the mocha-flavoured cake mixture in one half of the tin. Position the strip of foil down the centre, then spoon the hazelnut-flavoured cake mixture into the other half of the tin. Smooth the surface of both mixtures.

5 Bake for 30–35 minutes or until a skewer inserted into the centre of both halves comes out clean. Leave the cakes to cool in the tin for about 5 minutes, then turn out on to a wire rack, peel off the lining paper and leave to cool completely.

6 ▲ Separate the cakes and cut each one in half lengthways. Take one portion of the mocha-flavoured cake and brush along one long side with a little apricot jam. Sandwich this surface with a portion of the hazelnut-flavoured cake. Brush the top of the cakes with apricot jam and position the other portion of mocha-flavoured cake on top of the hazelnut base. Brush along the inner long side with apricot jam and sandwich with the final portion of hazelnut-flavoured cake. Set aside.

7 Knead the marzipan on the work surface to soften, then knead in the ground hazelnuts until evenly blended. On the work surface lightly dusted with icing sugar, roll out the marzipan into a rectangle large enough to wrap around the cake, excluding the ends.

8 Brush the long sides of the cake with apricot jam, then lay the cake on top of the marzipan. Wrap the marzipan around the cake, sealing the edge neatly. Place the cake on a serving plate, seal-side down, and pinch the edges of the marzipan to give an attractive finish. Score the top surface with a knife and sprinkle with ground hazelnuts.

Fresh Fruit Genoese

This Italian classic, 'Genovese con Panne e Frutta', can be made with any type of soft fresh fruit.

INGREDIENTS
Serves 8–10
For the Sponge
175 g/6 oz/1½ cups plain flour, sifted
pinch of salt
4 size 3 eggs
115 g/4 oz/½ cup caster sugar
6 tbsp orange-flavoured liqueur

For the Filling and Topping
600 ml/1 pint/2½ cups double cream
4 tbsp vanilla sugar
450 g/1 lb fresh soft fruit, such as raspberries, blueberries, cherries, etc.
150 g/5 oz/1¼ cups shelled pistachio nuts, finely chopped
4 tbsp apricot jam, warmed and sieved, to glaze

STORING
This cake is not suitable for storing.

To save time and money, use shop-bought chopped mixed nuts to coat the sides of the gâteau instead of pistachios.

1 Preheat the oven to 180°C/350°F/Gas 4. Grease a 21 cm/8½ inch round springform cake tin, line the base with greaseproof paper and grease the paper.

2 ▲ Sift the flour and salt together three times, then set aside.

3 Place the eggs and sugar in a mixing bowl and beat with an electric mixer for about 10 minutes or until thick and pale.

4 ▲ Sift the reserved flour mixture into the mixing bowl, then fold in very gently. Transfer the cake mixture to the prepared tin. Bake in the centre of the oven for 30–35 minutes or until a skewer inserted into the centre of the cake comes out clean. Leave the cake in the tin for about 5 minutes, then turn out on to a wire rack, peel off the lining paper and leave to cool completely.

5 Cut the cake horizontally into two layers, and place the bottom layer on a serving plate. Sprinkle the orange-flavoured liqueur over both layers.

6 ▲ Place the double cream and vanilla sugar in a mixing bowl and beat with an electric mixer until it holds peaks.

7 ▲ Spread two-thirds of the cream mixture over the bottom layer of cake and top with half the fruit. Place the second layer of the cake on top and spread the remaining cream over the top and sides.

8 Using a knife, lightly press the chopped nuts evenly around the sides. Arrange the remaining fresh fruit on top and brush over a light glaze using the apricot jam.

Chocolate Gâteau Terrine

A spectacular finale to a special-occasion meal. You'll find this is well worth the time and effort to make.

INGREDIENTS

Serves 10–12

115 g/4 oz/½ cup butter, softened
few drops of vanilla essence
115 g/4 oz/½ cup caster sugar
2 size 3 eggs
115 g/4 oz/1 cup self-raising flour, sifted
50 ml/2 fl oz/¼ cup milk
25 g/1 oz/½ cup desiccated coconut, to decorate
fresh bud roses, or other flowers, to decorate

For the Light Chocolate Filling

115 g/4 oz/½ cup butter, softened
2 tbsp icing sugar, sifted
75 g/3 oz/3 squares plain chocolate, melted
225 ml/8 fl oz/1 cup double cream, lightly whipped

For the Dark Chocolate Filling

115 g/4 oz/4 squares plain chocolate, chopped
115 g/4 oz/½ cup butter
2 size 3 eggs
2 tbsp caster sugar
225 ml/8 fl oz/1 cup double cream, lightly whipped
50 g/2 oz/½ cup cocoa powder
1 tbsp dark rum (optional)
2 tbsp gelatine powder dissolved in 2 tbsp hot water

For the White Chocolate Topping

225 g/8 oz/8 squares white chocolate
115 g/4 oz/½ cup butter

STORING

This cake is not suitable for storing.

1 Preheat the oven to 180°C/350°F/Gas 4. Grease a 900 g/2 lb loaf tin, line the base and sides with greaseproof paper and grease the paper.

2 To make the cake, place the butter, vanilla essence and sugar in a mixing bowl and beat until light and fluffy. Add the eggs, one at a time, beating well after each addition. Sift the flour again and fold it and the milk into the cake mixture.

3 Transfer the cake mixture to the prepared tin and bake in the centre of the oven for 25–30 minutes or until a skewer inserted into the centre of the cake comes out clean. Leave the cake in the tin for about 5 minutes, then turn out on to a wire rack, peel off the lining paper and leave to cool completely.

4 ▲ To make the light chocolate filling, place the butter and icing sugar in a mixing bowl and beat until creamy. Add the chocolate and cream until evenly blended. Cover and set aside in the refrigerator, until required.

5 To make the dark chocolate filling, place the chocolate and butter in a small saucepan and heat very gently, stirring frequently, until melted. Set aside to cool. Place the eggs and sugar in a bowl and beat with an electric mixer until thick and frothy. Fold in the cream, cocoa, rum and dissolved gelatine until evenly blended.

6 ▲ To assemble the terrine, wash and dry the loaf tin, then line with clear film, allowing plenty of film to hang over the edges. Using a long serrated knife, cut the cake horizontally into three even layers.

7 ▲ Spread two of the layers with the light chocolate filling, then place one of these layers, filling side up, in the base of the tin.

8 Cover with half of the dark chocolate filling, then chill for about 10 minutes. Place the second light chocolate-topped layer in the terrine, filling side up. Spread over the remaining dark chocolate filling, then chill for another 10 minutes. Top with the remaining layer of cake and chill the terrine again for about 10 minutes.

9 To make the white chocolate topping, place the chocolate and butter in a small saucepan and heat very gently, stirring frequently, until melted and well blended. Allow to cool slightly.

10 To finish the terrine, turn it out on to a wire rack, removing the clear film. Trim the edges with a long, sharp knife, then pour over the white chocolate topping, spreading it evenly over the sides. Sprinkle the coconut over the top and sides. Allow to set before transferring the terrine to a serving plate and decorating with fresh bud roses.

Vegan Dundee Cake

Containing no eggs or other dairy products, this cake is a rare treat for vegans. There are several different types of dairy-free margarines on the market, many of which are suitable for baking.

INGREDIENTS

Serves 8–10

350 g/12 oz/3 cups plain wholemeal flour
1 tsp ground mixed spice
175 g/6 oz/¾ cup vegan (soya) margarine
175 g/6 oz/¾ cup plus 2 tbsp dark muscavado sugar
175 g/6 oz/1 cup sultanas
175 g/6 oz/1 cup currants
175 g/6 oz/1 cup raisins
75 g/3 oz/⅔ cup chopped mixed peel
150 g/5 oz/⅔ glacé cherries, halved
finely grated zest of 1 orange
2 tbsp ground almonds
25 g/1 oz/¼ cup blanched almonds, chopped
125 ml/4 fl oz/½ cup soya milk
75 ml/3 fl oz/6 tbsp sunflower oil
2 tbsp malt vinegar
1 tsp bicarbonate of soda

To Decorate

mixed nuts, such as pistachios, pecans and macadamia, glacé cherries and angelica
4 tbsp clear honey, warmed

STORING

This cake can be kept for up to one week in an airtight container.

1 Preheat the oven to 150°C/300°F/ Gas 2. Grease a deep 20 cm/8 inch square loose-bottom cake tin, line with a double thickness of greaseproof paper and grease the paper.

2 ▲ Sift the flour and mixed spice into a large mixing bowl, adding the bran left in the sieve. Rub the margarine into the flour until it resembles fine breadcrumbs. Stir in the sugar, dried fruits, mixed peel, cherries, orange zest and ground and blanched almonds.

3 ▲ Warm 50 ml/2 fl oz/¼ cup of the soya milk in a saucepan, then add the sunflower oil and vinegar. Dissolve the bicarbonate of soda in the rest of the milk, then combine the two mixtures and stir into the dry ingredients.

4 ▲ Spoon the cake mixture into the prepared tin and smooth the surface. Bake in the centre of the oven for about 2½ hours or until a skewer inserted into the centre of the cake comes out clean. Leave the cake in the tin for about 5 minutes, then turn out on to a wire rack, peel off the lining paper and leave to cool completely.

5 Place the mixed nuts, glacé cherries and angelica on top of the cake, then brush with the warmed honey.

Autumn Cake

Greengages, plums or stoned semi-dried prunes are delicious in this recipe.

INGREDIENTS
Serves 6–8
115 g/4 oz/½ cup butter, softened
150 g/5 oz/¾ cup caster sugar
3 size 3 eggs, beaten
75 g/3 oz/1 cup ground hazelnuts
150 g/5 oz/1¼ cup shelled pecan nuts, chopped
50 g/2 oz/½ cup plain flour
1 tsp baking powder
½ tsp salt
675 g/1½ lb stoned plums, greengages or semi-dried prunes
4 tbsp lime marmalade
1 tbsp lime juice
2 tbsp blanched almonds, chopped, to decorate

STORING
This cake is not suitable for storing.

1 Preheat the oven to 180°C/350°F/ Gas 4. Grease a 23 cm/9 inch round, fluted tart tin.

2 ▲ Place the butter and sugar in a mixing bowl and beat with an electric mixer until light and fluffy. Gradually beat in the eggs, alternating with the ground hazelnuts, until evenly combined.

3 Stir in the pecan nuts, then sift in the flour, baking powder and salt. Fold in until evenly combined, then transfer the mixture to the prepared tin.

4 ▲ Bake in the centre of the oven for 45–50 minutes or until a skewer inserted into the centre of the cake comes out clean.

5 ▲ Remove from the oven and carefully arrange the fruit on top. Return to the oven and bake for a further 10–15 minutes until the fruit has softened. Transfer to a wire rack to cool completely then remove the cake from the tin.

6 Place the marmalade and lime juice in a small saucepan and warm gently. Brush over the fruit, then sprinkle with the almonds. Allow to set, then chill before serving.

Greek New Year Cake

A gold coin wrapped in foil is baked into this cake and tradition holds that good luck will come to the person who finds it.

INGREDIENTS
Serves 8–10
275 g/10 oz/2½ cups plain flour
2 tsp baking powder
50 g/2 oz/⅔ cup ground almonds
225 g/8 oz/1 cup butter, softened
175 g/6 oz/¾ cup plus 2 tbsp caster sugar, plus a little extra
4 size 3 eggs
150 ml/¼ pint/⅔ cup fresh orange juice
50 g/2 oz/½ cup blanched almonds
1 tbsp sesame seeds

STORING
This cake can be kept for up to four days in an airtight container.

1 ▲ Preheat the oven to 180°C/350°F/ Gas 4. Grease a 23 cm/9 inch square cake tin, line the base and sides with greaseproof paper and grease the paper.

2 ▲ Sift the flour and baking powder into a mixing bowl and stir in the ground almonds.

3 ▲ In another mixing bowl, cream together the butter and sugar until light and fluffy. Beat in the eggs, one at a time, using an electric mixer. Fold in the flour mixture, alternating with the orange juice, until evenly combined.

4 ▲ Add a coin wrapped in foil if you wish to make the cake in the traditional manner, then spoon the cake mixture into the prepared tin and smooth the surface. Arrange the almonds on top, then sprinkle over the sesame seeds. Bake in the centre of the oven for 50–55 minutes or until a skewer inserted into the centre of the cake comes out clean. Leave to cool in the tin for about 5 minutes, then turn out on to a wire rack, peel off the lining paper and leave to cool completely. Serve cut into diamond shapes.

Upside-down Pear & Ginger Cake

A light spicy sponge topped with glossy baked fruit and ginger. This is also good served warm for pudding.

INGREDIENTS

Serves 6–8

1 x 900 g/2 lb can pear halves, drained
8 tbsp finely chopped stem ginger
8 tbsp ginger syrup from the jar
175 g/6 oz/1½ cups self-raising flour
½ tsp baking powder
1 tsp ground ginger
175 g/6 oz/¾ cup soft light brown sugar
175 g/6 oz/¾ cup butter, softened
3 size 3 eggs, lightly beaten

STORING

This cake is not suitable for storing.

1 Preheat the oven to 180°C/350°F/Gas 4. Grease a deep 20 cm/8 inch round cake tin, line the base with greaseproof paper and grease the paper.

2 ▲ Fill the hollow in each pear with half the chopped ginger. Arrange the pear halves, flat sides down, over the base of the cake tin, then spoon half the ginger syrup over the top.

3 Sift the flour, baking powder and ground ginger into a mixing bowl. Stir in the soft brown sugar and butter, then add the eggs and beat together for 1–2 minutes until level and creamy.

4 ▲ Carefully spoon the mixture into the tin and smooth the surface.

5 ▲ Bake in the centre of the oven for about 50 minutes, or until a skewer inserted in the centre of the cake comes out clean. Leave the cake to cool in the tin for about 5 minutes. Turn out on to a wire rack, peel off the lining paper and leave to cool completely. Add the reserved chopped ginger to the pear halves and drizzle over the remaining ginger syrup.

Marbled Spice Cake

This cake is baked in a fluted ring-shaped tin called a kugelhupf, or gugelhupf, mould from Germany and Austria to give it a pretty shape.

INGREDIENTS

Serves 8–10

75 g/3 oz/6 tbsp butter, softened
115 g/4 oz/½ cup caster sugar
2 size 3 eggs, lightly beaten
few drops of vanilla essence
130 g/4½ oz plain flour
1½ tsp baking powder
3 tbsp milk
3 tbsp black treacle
1 tsp ground mixed spice
½ tsp ground ginger
175 g/6 oz/1⅛ cups icing sugar, sifted, to decorate

STORING

This cake can be kept for up to two days in an airtight container.

1 Preheat the oven to 180°C/350°F/ Gas 4. Grease and flour a 900 g/2 lb kugelhupf mould or ring-shaped cake tin.

2 Cream the butter and sugar together in a bowl until light and fluffy. Beat in the egg and vanilla essence.

3 ▲ Sift together the flour and baking powder, then fold into the mixture, alternating with the milk, until evenly combined.

4 Spoon about one-third of the mixture into a small bowl and stir in the treacle and spices.

5 ▲ Drop alternating spoonfuls of the light and dark mixtures into the tin. Run a knife or skewer through them to give a marbled effect.

6 ▲ Bake in the centre of the oven for about 50 minutes or until a skewer inserted into the centre comes out clean. Leave in the tin for 10 minutes before turning out on to a wire rack to cool.

7 ▲ To decorate, stir enough warm water into the icing sugar to make a smooth icing. Spoon quickly over the cake. Allow to set before serving.

Tip

If you do not have a kugelhupf mould or a ring-shaped cake tin, use a 20 cm/8 inch round cake tin.

Apricot Brandy-snap Roulade

A magnificent combination of soft and crisp textures, this cake looks impressive and is easy to prepare.

INGREDIENTS

Serves 6–8

4 size 3 eggs, separated
1/2 tbsp fresh orange juice
115 g/4 oz/1/2 cup caster sugar
175 g/6 oz/2 cups ground almonds
4 brandy-snap biscuits, crushed, to decorate

For the Filling

150 g/5 oz canned apricots, drained
300 ml/1/2 pint/1 1/4 cups double cream
25 g/1 oz/4 tbsp icing sugar

STORING

This cake is not suitable for storing.

1 ▲ Preheat the oven to 190°C/375°F/ Gas 5. Grease a 33 x 23 cm/13 x 9 inch Swiss roll tin, line the base with greaseproof paper and grease the paper.

2 Place the egg yolks, orange juice and sugar in a mixing bowl and beat with an electric mixer for about 10 minutes until thick and pale. Fold in the ground almonds.

3 ▲ Whisk the egg whites until they hold stiff peaks. Fold the egg whites into the almond mixture, then transfer to the Swiss roll tin and smooth the surface. Bake in the centre of the oven for about 20 minutes or until a skewer inserted into the centre comes out clean. Leave to cool in the tin, covered with a clean, just-damp cloth.

4 ▲ To make the filling, place the apricots in a blender or food processor and purée until smooth. Place the cream and icing sugar in a mixing bowl and whip until the cream holds soft peaks. Fold in the apricot purée.

5 Spread out the crushed brandy-snaps, on a sheet of greaseproof paper. Spread about one-third of the cream mixture over the cake, then invert it on to the crushed brandy-snaps. Peel away the lining paper.

6 Use the remaining cream mixture to cover the cake, then, using the greaseproof paper as a guide, tightly and neatly roll up the roulade from a short end. Transfer to a serving dish, sticking on any extra pieces of crushed brandy-snaps.

Apple Crumble Cake

In the autumn use windfall apples. Served warm with thick cream or custard this cake doubles as a dessert.

INGREDIENTS

Serves 8-10

For the Topping

75 g/3 oz/¾ cup self-raising flour
½ tsp ground cinnamon
40 g/1½ oz/3 tbsp butter
25 g/1 oz/2 tbsp caster sugar

For the Base

50 g/2 oz/4 tbsp butter, softened
75 g/3 oz/6 tbsp caster sugar
1 size 3 egg, beaten
115 g/4 oz/1 cup self-raising flour, sifted
2 cooking apples, peeled, cored and sliced
50 g/2 oz/⅓ cup sultanas

To Decorate

1 red dessert apple, cored, thinly sliced and tossed in lemon juice
2 tbsp caster sugar, sifted
pinch of ground cinnamon

STORING

This cake can be kept for up to two days in an airtight container.

1 Preheat the oven 180°C/350°F/Gas 4. Grease a deep 18 cm/7 inch springform tin, line the base with greaseproof paper and grease the paper.

2 ▲ To make the topping, sift the flour and cinnamon into a mixing bowl. Rub the butter into the flour until it resembles breadcrumbs, then stir in the sugar. Set aside.

3 ▲ To make the base, put the butter, sugar, egg and flour into a bowl and beat for 1–2 minutes until smooth . Spoon into the prepared tin.

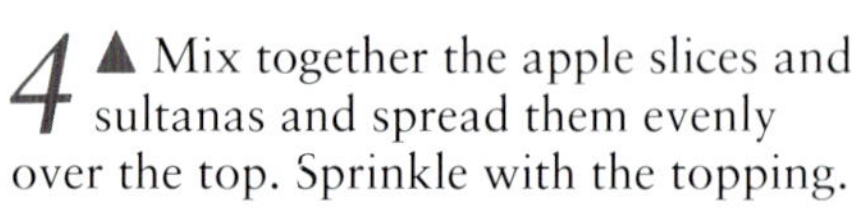

4 ▲ Mix together the apple slices and sultanas and spread them evenly over the top. Sprinkle with the topping.

5 Bake in the centre of the oven for about 1 hour. Cool in the tin for 10 minutes before turning out on to a wire rack and peeling off the lining paper. Serve warm or cool, decorated with slices of red dessert apple and caster sugar and cinnamon sprinkled over.

Summer Strawberry Shortcake

A summer-time treat. Serve with a cool glass of pink sparkling wine for a truly refreshing dessert.

Ingredients

Serves 6–8

225 g/8 oz/2 cups plain flour
1 tbsp baking powder
½ tsp salt
50 g/2 oz/4 tbsp caster sugar
50 g/2 oz/4 tbsp butter, softened
150 ml/¼ pint/⅔ cup milk
300 ml/½ pint/1¼ cups double cream
450 g/1 lb fresh strawberries, halved and hulled

STORING

This cake is not suitable for storing.

1 Preheat the oven to 220°C/425°F/ Gas 7. Grease a baking sheet, line the base with greaseproof paper and grease the paper.

2 ▲ Sift the flour, baking powder and salt together into a large mixing bowl. Stir in the sugar, cut in the butter and toss into the flour mixture until it resembles coarse breadcrumbs. Stir in just enough milk to make a soft dough.

3 ▲ Turn out the dough on to a lightly floured work surface and pat, using your fingers, into a 30 x 15 cm/12 x 6 inch rectangle. Using a template, cut out two 15 cm/6 inch rounds, indent one of the rounds dividing it into eight equal portions, and place them on the baking sheet.

4 ▲ Bake in the centre of the oven for 10–15 minutes or until slightly risen and golden. Leave the shortcake on the baking sheet for about 5 minutes, then transfer to a wire rack, peel off the lining paper and leave to cool completely.

5 Place the cream in a mixing bowl and whip with an electric mixer until it holds soft peaks. Place the unmarked shortcake on a serving plate and spread or pipe with half of the cream. Top with two-thirds of the strawberries, then the other shortcake. Use the remaining cream and strawberries to decorate the top layer. Chill for at least 30 minutes before serving.

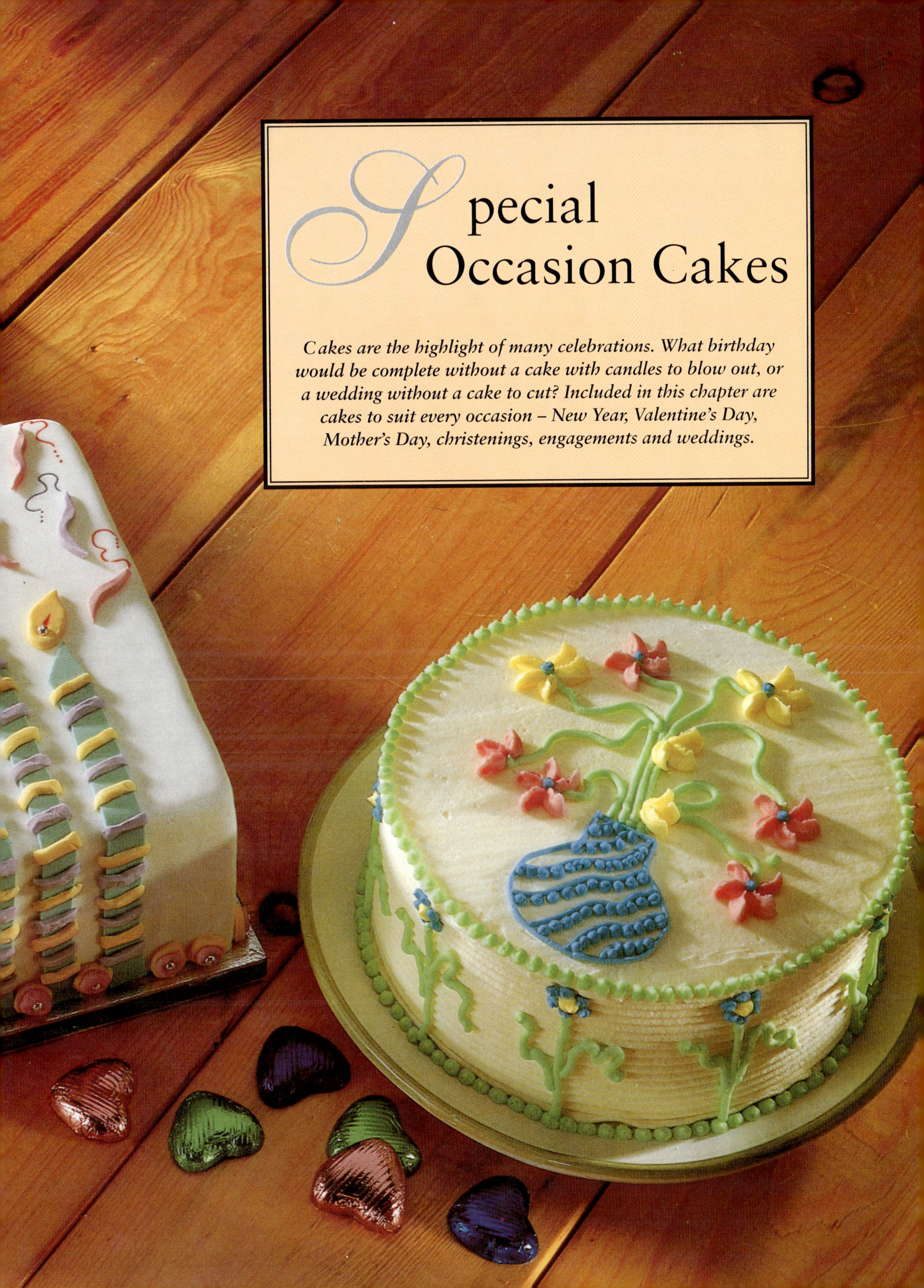

Special Occasion Cakes

Cakes are the highlight of many celebrations. What birthday would be complete without a cake with candles to blow out, or a wedding without a cake to cut? Included in this chapter are cakes to suit every occasion – New Year, Valentine's Day, Mother's Day, christenings, engagements and weddings.

Teddy Bear Christening Cake

To personalise the cake, make a simple plaque for the top and pipe or write the name of the new baby with a food colouring pen.

Ingredients

Serves 30

20 cm/8 inch square Light Fruit Cake

3 tbsp apricot jam, warmed and sieved

900 g/2 lb marzipan

800 g/1¾ lb/2⅓ x quantity Sugarpaste Icing

peach, yellow, blue and brown food colourings

115 g/4oz/⅙ quantity Royal Icing

MATERIALS AND EQUIPMENT

25 cm/10 inch square cake board

crimping tool

blossom cutter or plunger

foam pad

7.5 cm/3 inch round cutter

frill cutter

wooden cocktail stick

peach ribbon

small blue ribbon bow

STORING

The finished cake can be stored for up to four weeks in an airtight container.

1 Brush the cake with the apricot jam. Roll out the marzipan on a work surface lightly dusted with icing sugar, then use to cover the cake. Leave to dry for 12 hours.

2 Colour 500 g/1¼ lb of the sugarpaste icing peach. Roll out the icing. Brush the marzipan with a little water and cover the cake with the icing.

3 ▲ Position the cake on the cake board. Using a crimping tool dipped in cornflour, crimp the top and bottom edges of the cake.

4 Divide the remaining sugarpaste into three portions. Leave one-third white and colour one-third yellow. Cut the remaining third in half and colour one portion peach and the other blue.

5 ▲ To make the flowers, roll out the peach and blue sugarpaste thinly on a work surface lightly dusted with icing sugar. Dip the end of the blossom cutter or a plunger in cornflour and cut out small and larger flowers. Place a small ball of peach icing in the centre of the blue flowers; and a small ball of blue icing in the centre of the peach flowers. Secure with water, if necessary. Leave the flowers to dry on a foam pad for several hours or overnight. Gather together the blue icing trimmings and set aside, wrapped in clear film.

6 ▲ Make the teddy bear with the yellow icing. Shape the head, body, arms and ears of the bear and press together with a little water to secure. Make the button for the chest out of a little blue icing. Paint on highlights, such as eyes, nose and mouth, with brown food colouring. Leave the bear to dry on a piece of greaseproof paper for several hours or overnight.

7 To make the blanket, roll out the blue icing and cut out a circle with the 7.5 cm/3 inch round cutter. Slice off a small piece, about 1 cm/½ inch, to give a straight line for the top. Set aside. Roll out the white icing thinly and, using the frill cutter, cut out a ring. Put the end of the wooden cocktail stick over about 5 mm/¼ inch of the outer edge of the ring. Roll the stick around the edge firmly back and forth with your finger so the edge becomes thinner and begins to frill. Continue until the ring is completely frilled. Using a sharp knife, cut through the ring once to open it up. Gently ease it open.

8 ▲ Brush the edge of the blue blanket with water and secure the white frill on to the edge.

9 Decorate the cake with the ribbon. Position the bear on top and lay the blanket over it, securing with a little water or royal icing. Secure the flowers with a little royal icing and then the bow to the bear's neck in the same way.

Jazzy Chocolate Gâteau

This cake is made with Father's Day in mind, though really it can be made for anyone who loves chocolate.

Ingredients
Serves 12–15
2 x quantity chocolate-flavour Quick-Mix Sponge Cake mix
75 g/3 oz/3 squares plain chocolate
75 g/3 oz/3 squares white chocolate
½ quantity Fudge Frosting
½ quantity Glacé Icing
1 tsp weak coffee
8 tbsp chocolate hazelnut spread

MATERIALS AND EQUIPMENT
2 x 20 cm/8 inch round cake tins
greaseproof paper piping bag
No 1 writing nozzle

STORING
The finished cake can be kept for up to three days in the fridge.

1 Preheat the oven to 160°C/325°F/ Gas 3. Grease the cake tins, line the bases with greaseproof paper and grease the paper. Divide the cake mixture evenly between the tins and smooth the surfaces. Bake in the centre of the oven for 20–30 minutes, or until firm to the touch. Turn out on to a wire rack, peel off the lining paper and leave to cool completely.

2 Meanwhile, cover a large baking sheet or board (or two smaller ones) with baking parchment and tape it down at each corner. Melt each chocolate in separate bowls over pans of hot water, stirring until smooth, then pour on to the baking parchment. Spread out the chocolates evenly with a palette knife. Allow to cool until the surfaces are firm enough to cut, but not so hard that they will break. The chocolate should no longer feel sticky when touched with your finger.

3 ▲ Cut out haphazard shapes of chocolate and set aside.

4 ▲ Make the fudge frosting and, when cool enough to spread, use to sandwich the two cakes together. Place the cake on a stand or plate.

5 Make the glacé icing, using 1 tsp weak coffee (to colour it very slightly) along with enough water to form a spreading consistency, and spread on top of the cake almost to the edges. Spread the side of the cake with enough chocolate hazelnut spread to cover.

6 ▲ Arrange the chocolate pieces around the side of the cake, pressing into the hazelnut spread to secure.

7 To decorate, spoon about 3 tbsp of the chocolate hazelnut spread into a piping bag fitted with a No 1 nozzle and pipe 'jazzy' lines over the glacé icing.

Mother's Day Bouquet

A piped bouquet of flowers can bring as much pleasure as a fresh one for a Mother's Day treat.

INGREDIENTS
Serves 8–10
1 quantity Quick-Mix Sponge Cake mix
2 x quantity Butter Icing
green, blue, yellow and pink food colourings

MATERIALS AND EQUIPMENT
2 x 18 cm/7 inch round cake tins
serrated scraper
5 greaseproof paper piping bags
No 3 writing and petal nozzles

STORING
The finished cake can be kept for up to three days in an airtight container in the fridge.

1 Preheat the oven to 160°C/325°F/ Gas 3. Grease the cake tins, line the bases with greaseproof paper and grease the paper. Divide the cake mixture evenly between the tins and smooth the surfaces. Bake in the centre of the oven for about 20 minutes or until firm to the touch. Turn out on to a wire rack, peel off the lining paper and leave to cool.

2 ▲ Place one of the cakes on paper on a turntable. Use half to two-thirds of the butter icing to sandwich the cakes together and to coat the top and sides. Coat the top using a palette knife and the sides using the scraper.

3 Transfer the cake to a serving plate, then divide the remaining butter icing into four bowls and colour one portion green, one portion blue, one portion yellow and one portion pink. Spoon the blue icing into a greaseproof paper piping bag fitted with the No 3 writing nozzle. Pipe the vase on top of the cake in lines and beads.

4 ▲ Spoon the green icing into a fresh piping bag fitted with a clean No 3 writing nozzle. Pipe the flower stems coming out of the vase.

5 Spoon the pink icing into a fresh piping bag fitted with the petal nozzle. Pipe pink petals on the ends of some of the stems. Pipe beads of blue icing in the centres.

6 Spoon most of the yellow icing into a fresh piping bag fitted with a clean petal nozzle and pipe yellow flowers on the remaining stems. Pipe beads of blue icing in the centres.

7 ▲ Decorate the side of the cake. Pipe stems with leaves evenly spaced all around the side with the green icing, and pipe beads of the blue icing to make flowers at the end of each stem. Spoon the reserved yellow icing into a fresh piping bag fitted with a clean No 3 writing nozzle and pipe small beads in the centre of the blue flowers.

8 Pipe beads of green icing round the top and bottom edges of the cake.

Flickering Birthday Candle Cake

Stripy icing candles are flickering and ready to blow out on this birthday celebration cake for all ages.

INGREDIENTS
Serves 15–20
20 cm/8 inch square Madeira Cake
1 quantity Butter Icing
3 tbsp apricot jam, warmed and sieved
800 g/1¾ lb/2⅓ x quantity Sugarpaste Icing
pink, yellow, purple and jade food colourings
edible silver balls, to decorate

MATERIALS AND EQUIPMENT
23 cm/9 inch square cake board
leaf cutter
small round cutter
pink and purple food colouring pens
5 mm/¼ inch wide jade-coloured ribbon

STORING
The finished cake can be kept for up to one week in an airtight container.

1 Cut the cake horizontally into three layers, using a long serrated knife. Sandwich the layers together with the butter icing and brush the cake with the apricot jam. Roll out 500 g/1¼ lb of the sugarpaste icing on a work surface lightly dusted with icing sugar and use to cover the cake. Position on the cake board.

2 Divide the remaining sugarpaste into four portions and colour one portion pink, one portion yellow, one portion pale purple and one portion jade. Roll out the jade icing and cut into six 1 cm/½ inch wide strips of slightly different lengths, but each long enough to go over the side and on to the top of the cake. Make a diagonal cut at one end of each strip.

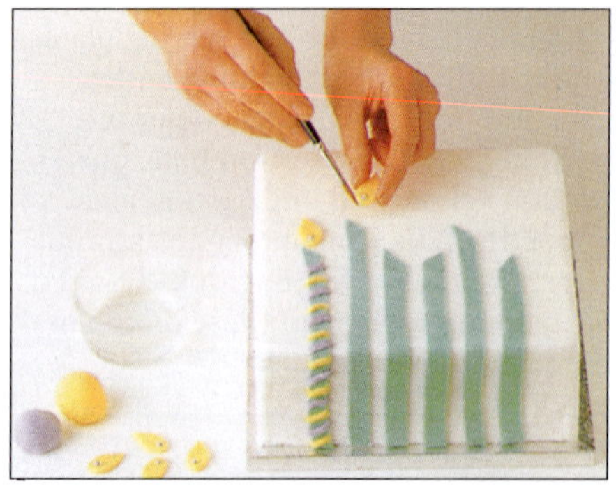

3 ▲ Roll out the yellow icing and cut out six candle flames with the leaf cutter. Place a silver ball in each flame. Set aside the remaining yellow icing, wrapped in clear film. Arrange the candles on top of the cake, securing with a little water. Mould small strips, fractionally longer than the width of each candle, from the yellow and purple icings. Arrange alternate colours on the candles at a slight angle, securing with water. Position the flames at the end of each jade strip, also securing with water.

4 ▲ Roll out the pink and remaining purple icings, then cut out wavy pieces with a sharp knife. Attach to the cake, above the candles, with a little water. Gather together the pink icing trimmings and roll into a ball.

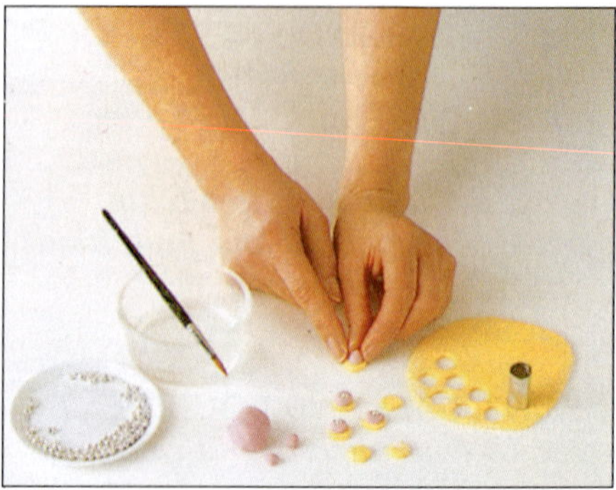

5 ▲ Using the leftover yellow and pink icings, make the decorations for the sides of the cake. Roll out the yellow icing and cut out circles with the small round cutter or the end of a piping nozzle. Make small balls from the pink icing and attach to the yellow circles with a little water. Press a silver ball in the centre of each pink ball.

6 Arrange the decorations around the bottom edge of the cake, securing with water.

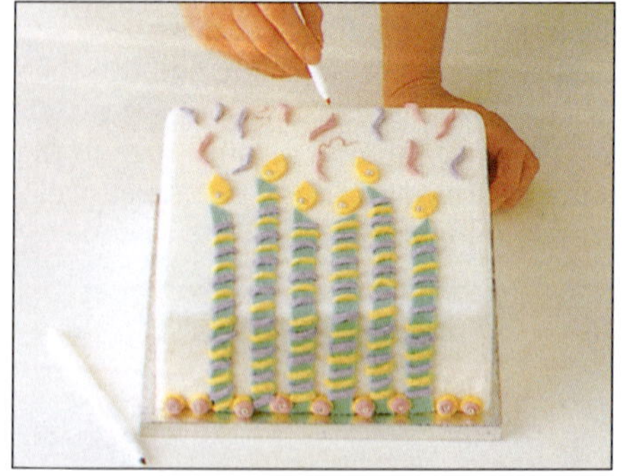

7 ▲ Using food colouring pens, draw wavy lines and dots coming from the purple and pink wavy icings. Decorate the sides of the cake board with the ribbon, securing at the back with a little softened sugarpaste.

Harvest Blackberry Ring

Gracious blackberry branches twisting their way over the cake, and leaves tinged with reddish-brown, create an autumnal theme.

Ingredients
Serves 20
1 quantity 18 cm/7 inch round Light Fruit Cake mix
3 tbsp apricot jam, warmed and sieved
450 g/1 lb marzipan
900 g/2 lb/2²/₃ x quantity Sugarpaste Icing
tangerine, purple, green and paprika food colourings

MATERIALS AND EQUIPMENT
20 cm/8 inch ring mould
25 cm/10 inch round cake board

STORING
The finished cake can be kept for up to four weeks in an airtight container.

1 Preheat the oven to 150°C/300°f/ Gas 2. Grease the cake tin, line with greaseproof paper and grease the paper. Spoon in the cake mixture and smooth the surface with the back of a wet metal spoon. Bake in the centre of the oven for 1½–2 hours or until a skewer inserted in the centre of the cake comes out clean. Leave the cake to cool in the mould on a wire rack. When completely cool, turn out.

2 Brush the cake with the apricot jam. Measure half the circumference of the cake with a piece of string. Measure the height to include the top as well as the sides of the cake (see step 4 for guidance). Take three-quarters of the marzipan and cut in half. Cover the cake in two halves as follows. Roll out each piece of marzipan on a work surface lightly dusted with icing sugar and trim each using the string measurements as a guide. Trim and press the joins together to secure.

3 Measure the height and circumference of the inside of the ring with string. Cover the inside by rolling out the remaining one-quarter of marzipan. Trim to fit and press the joins together to secure. Position the cake on the board. Leave to dry for 12 hours.

4 ▲ Measure half the circumference of the cake with a piece of string. Measure the height to include the top as well as the sides of the cake.

5 ▲ Colour 675 g/1½ lb of the sugarpaste icing pale tangerine. Cut off three-quarters of this and cut in half. Keep the remaining icing well wrapped. Brush the marzipan lightly with water. Cover the top and sides of the cake in two pieces by rolling out each piece of icing. Trim and press the joins together.

6 Measure the height and circumference of the inside of the ring with string. Cover the inside of the ring by rolling out the remaining one-quarter of sugarpaste icing, using the string measurement as a guide. Trim to fit and press the joins together to secure.

7 ▲ Colour one-quarter of the white sugarpaste icing purple. To mould the blackberries, take a little of the purple icing and form into balls of different sizes for the bases. Make a number of smaller balls and stick them on the outside of the larger ones, securing with water. Place on a piece of greaseproof paper and leave to dry while making the leaves and branches.

8 ▲ Colour two-thirds of the remaining white sugarpaste icing green and the rest paprika. Reserve half of the green icing for the stems, and knead the remaining green and the paprika icing lightly together until marbled. Roll out and cut out leaf shapes. Make the branches by rolling the green icing into long thin strands.

9 To assemble, arrange the branches on the cake, securing them with a little water and twisting them as necessary, covering any joins in the icing where possible. Attach the leaves, bending them into shape, then arrange the blackberries on the cake attaching all with a little water.

Double Heart Engagement Cake

For a celebratory engagement party, these sumptuous cakes make the perfect centrepiece.

Ingredients

Serves 20

2 x quantity chocolate-flavour Quick-Mix Sponge Cake mix
350 g/12 oz/12 squares plain chocolate
2 x quantity coffee-flavour Butter Icing
icing sugar, for sifting
fresh raspberries, to decorate

MATERIALS AND EQUIPMENT

2 x 20 cm/8 inch heart-shaped cake tins
2 x 23 cm/9 inch heart-shaped cake boards

STORING

The finished cakes can be kept for up to three days in an airtight container in the fridge.

1 Preheat the oven to 160°C/325°F/ Gas 3. Grease the tins, line the bases with greaseproof paper and grease the paper. Divide the cake mixture evenly between the tins and smooth the surfaces. Bake in the centre of the oven for 25–30 minutes or until firm to the touch. Turn out on to a wire rack, peel off the lining paper and leave to cool completely.

2 Meanwhile, melt the chocolate in a heatproof bowl over a saucepan of hot water (you may find it easier to work with half the chocolate at a time). Pour the melted chocolate on to a firm, smooth surface such as a marble or plastic laminate set on a slightly damp cloth to prevent slipping. Spread the chocolate out evenly with a large palette knife. Leave the chocolate to cool slightly. It should feel just set, but not hard.

3 ▲ To make the chocolate curls, hold a large sharp knife at a 45° angle to the chocolate and push it along the chocolate in short sawing movements from right to left and left to right. Remove the curls by sliding the point of the knife underneath each one and lifting off. Leave to firm on baking parchment. Repeat with remaining chocolate.

4 ▲ Cut each cake in half horizontally. Use about one-third of the butter icing to fill both cakes, then sandwich them together.

5 Use the remaining icing to coat the tops and sides of the cakes.

6 ▲ Place the cakes on the cake boards. Generously cover the tops and sides of the cakes with the chocolate curls, pressing them gently into the butter icing.

7 Sift a little icing sugar over the top of each cake and decorate with raspberries. Chill until ready to serve.

Coffee Almond Flower Gâteau

There are all kinds of reasons for making a cake for someone - sometimes it may be simply to say 'thank you'.

INGREDIENTS

Serves 8–10

1 quantity Quick-Mix Sponge Cake mix
25 g/1 oz/¼ cup nuts, such as almonds or walnuts, finely chopped
1½ x quantity coffee-flavour Butter Icing
75 g/3oz/3 squares plain chocolate
20 blanched almonds
4 chocolate-coated espresso beans

MATERIALS AND EQUIPMENT

2 x 18 cm/7 inch round cake tins
serrated scraper
2 greaseproof paper piping bags
No 2 writing nozzle

STORING

The finished cake can be kept for up to three days in an airtight container in the fridge.

1 Preheat the oven to 160°C/325°F/Gas 3. Grease the cake tins, line the bases with greaseproof paper and grease the paper. Fold the nuts into the cake mixture. Divide the mixture evenly between the tins and smooth the surfaces. Bake in the centre of the oven for about 20 minutes or until firm to the touch. Turn out on to a wire rack, peel off the lining paper and leave to cool completely.

2 Place one of the cakes on a piece of greaseproof paper on a turntable. Use the butter icing to sandwich the cakes together and to ice the top and side. Coat the top by spreading the icing smoothly with a palette knife. Coat the side with a serrated scraper. Reserve two spoonfuls of icing for piping.

3 ▲ Melt the chocolate in a heatproof bowl over a pan of hot water. Remove from the heat, then dip half of each almond into the chocolate at a slight angle. Shake off any excess chocolate and leave the almonds to dry on baking parchment. Return the chocolate to the pan of hot water (off the heat) so it does not set. Remove and allow to cool slightly before using for piping.

4 Arrange the almonds on top of the cake to represent flowers.

5 ▲ Place a chocolate-coated espresso bean in the centre of each almond flower. Spoon the remaining melted chocolate into a greaseproof paper piping bag. Cut a small piece off the end in a straight line. Pipe the chocolate in wavy lines over the top of the cake and in small beads around the top edge.

6 Transfer the cake to a cake stand or serving plate. Work quickly so the chocolate in the piping bag does not become too firm to pipe. Place the reserved butter icing in a fresh piping bag fitted with the No 2 writing nozzle. Pipe beads of icing all around the bottom of the cake, then top with small beads of chocolate, allowing the chocolate to drizzle on to the stand.

Pansy Retirement Cake

Sugar-frosted edible flowers make a very effective cake decoration. If pansies are not in season, use other edible flowers such as nasturtiums, roses or tiny daffodils to wish someone a happy retirement. Just co-ordinate the colour of the icing, piping and ribbon with the colour of the flowers.

Ingredients

Serves 20–25

20 cm/8 inch round Light Fruit Cake
3 tbsp apricot jam, warmed and sieved
675 g/1½ lb marzipan
1.1 kg/2½ lb/1⅔ x quantity Royal Icing
orange food colouring
1 size 3 egg white, lightly beaten
caster sugar, for frosting
about 7 pansies (orange and purple)

MATERIALS AND EQUIPMENT

25 cm/10 inch round cake board
2 greaseproof paper piping bags
No 19 star and No 1 writing nozzles
2 cm/¾ inch wide purple ribbon
3 mm/⅛ inch wide dark purple ribbon

STORING

The finished cake can be kept for up to four weeks in an airtight container.

1 Brush the cake with the apricot jam. Roll out the marzipan on a work surface lightly dusted with icing sugar and cover the cake. Leave to dry for 12 hours.

2 Secure the cake to the cake board with a little of the royal icing. Colour one-quarter of the royal icing pale orange. Flat ice the cake with three or four layers of smooth icing, allowing each layer to dry overnight before applying the next, using the orange icing for the top and the white for the sides. Set aside a little of both icings in airtight containers, to decorate the cake.

3 ▲ To sugar-frost the pansies, have ready a small bowl with the egg white and a plate with caster sugar. Dry the pansies on kitchen paper. If possible, leave some stem attached. Evenly brush the pansies all over on both sides of the petals with the egg white. Holding the flowers by their stems, sprinkle them evenly with the sugar, then shake off any excess. Place the frosted flowers on a flat board or wire rack covered with greaseproof or kitchen paper and leave to dry in a warm place overnight.

4 ▲ Spoon the reserved white royal icing into a greaseproof paper piping bag fitted with a No 19 star nozzle. Pipe a row of scrolls around the top of the cake.

5 ▲ Reverse the direction of the scrolls and pipe another row directly underneath the first row.

6 ▲ Pipe another row of scrolls around the bottom of the cake. Spoon the reserved orange icing into a fresh piping bag fitted with a No 1 writing nozzle. Pipe around the outline of the top of each scroll.

7 Using the same piping bag, pipe a row of single dots underneath the top row of reverse scrolls and a double row of dots above the bottom row of scrolls. Arrange the sugar-frosted pansies on top of the cake. Decorate with the ribbons, centring the narrow, darker ribbon on top of the wider one.

Valentine's Heart Cake

Cakes decorated with hearts can be very adaptable. Although this one was designed with Valentine's Day in mind, it could also be used to celebrate a birthday for someone special, an anniversary, or be made as two tiers for a wedding cake.

Ingredients

Serves 30
20 cm/8 inch square Light Fruit Cake
3 tbsp apricot jam, warmed and sieved
900 g/2 lb marzipan
1.5 kg/3 lb/2 x quantity Royal Icing
115 g/4 oz/1/3 quantity Sugarpaste Icing
red food colouring

MATERIALS AND EQUIPMENT
1 x 25 cm/10 inch square cake board
5 cm/2 inch heart-shaped cutter
2.5 cm/1 inch heart-shaped cutter
4 greaseproof paper piping bags
No 1 and No 2 writing and No 42 star nozzles
heart-patterned ribbon

STORING
The finished cake can be kept for up to four weeks in an airtight container.

1 Brush the cake with the apricot jam. Roll out the marzipan on a surface lightly dusted with icing sugar and cover the cake. Leave to dry for 12 hours.

2 Secure the cake to the cake board with a little of the royal icing. Flat ice the cake with three or four layers of smooth icing, allowing each layer to dry overnight before applying the next. Set aside a little of the royal icing in an airtight container for piping.

3 ▲ To make the heart decorations, colour the sugarpaste icing red. Roll out the red icing on a work surface lightly dusted with icing sugar and cut out 12 hearts with the 5 cm/2 inch heart-shaped cutter. Place the 2.5 cm/1 inch heart-shaped cutter in the centre of each larger heart and cut out a smaller heart, so you have 12 small hearts and 12 larger hollow hearts. Cut out four more smaller hearts from the red icing so you have 16 total. Place the hearts on a board covered with greaseproof paper.

4 ▲ Spoon a little of the reserved royal icing into a greaseproof paper piping bag fitted with a No 1 writing nozzle. Pipe wavy lines around the edges of four of the small hearts. Leave all the hearts to dry for several hours or overnight.

5 ▲ Spoon some more royal icing into a fresh piping bag fitted with a No 42 nozzle. Pipe swirls around the top and bottom edges of the cake with some of the royal icing.

6 ▲ Colour a heaped tablespoon of the remaining royal icing red and spoon into a fresh piping bag fitted with a clean No 1 writing nozzle. Pipe red dots on top of each white swirl of icing.

7 ▲ Arrange four of the large hearts on top of the cake, securing with a little royal icing.

8 Decorate with the ribbon. Spoon the remaining white royal icing into a fresh piping bag fitted with a No 2 writing nozzle. Pipe beads of icing down each side of the cake, above and below the ribbon. Allow all the piping to dry for several hours.

9 Arrange the remaining large hearts on top of the cake, securing with a little royal icing. Arrange the remaining small hearts on the sides.

Holly Leaf Log

Christmas cakes can be made in all shapes and sizes. This log-shaped cake is for chocolate and coffee lovers.

Ingredients
Serves 8
1 quantity Swiss Roll mix
½ quantity coffee-flavour Butter Icing
75 g/3 oz/3 squares plain chocolate
1½ x quantity Fudge Frosting

MATERIALS AND EQUIPMENT
Swiss roll tin
holly leaf cutter
2 greaseproof paper piping bags
No 1 writing and No 30 star nozzles

STORING
This cake can be kept for two days in the fridge in an airtight container.

1 Make and bake the Swiss roll. Turn out on to a sheet of greaseproof paper lightly sprinkled with caster sugar and roll up leaving the lining paper inside. Leave to cool completely on a wire rack.

2 ▲ Unroll the cake carefully and remove the paper. Reserve a spoonful of the butter icing for piping on the holly leaves, and spread the remainder over the cake. Re-roll the cake, place on a sheet of greaseproof paper on a wire rack and set aside.

3 To make the chocolate decorations, cover a baking sheet with baking parchment and tape it down at each corner. Melt the chocolate in a heatproof bowl over a pan of hot water, then pour on to the baking parchment.

4 Spread out the chocolate evenly with a palette knife, and allow to cool until the surface is firm enough to cut, but not so hard that it will break. The chocolate should no longer feel sticky when touched with your finger.

5 ▲ Press a holly leaf cutter firmly through the chocolate and lift off the leaves with a small palette knife. Spoon the reserved butter icing into a greaseproof paper piping bag fitted with the No 1 writing nozzle. Use to pipe decorations on the chocolate leaves.

6 ▲ Make the fudge frosting and, when cool enough to spread, quickly cover the Swiss roll with about two-thirds of the frosting. Working quickly before the frosting becomes too stiff, make swirls over the surface with a palette knife.

7 ▲ Spoon the remaining frosting into a fresh piping bag fitted with the No 30 star nozzle. Pipe several lines of scrolls down the length of the cake.

8 Transfer to a serving plate and arrange the chocolate leaves on the cake, pressing lightly to secure.

Starry New Year Cake

Although it is not so traditional to welcome in the New Year with a cake as it is at Christmas, why not start a new tradition?

INGREDIENTS

Serves 15–20

23 cm/9 inch round Madeira Cake
2 x quantity Butter Icing
800 g/1¾ lb/2⅓ x quantity Sugarpaste Icing
grape violet and mulberry food colourings
gold, lilac shimmer and primrose sparkle powdered food colourings

MATERIALS AND EQUIPMENT

star-shaped cutter
florist's wire
28 cm/11 inch round cake board
purple ribbon with gold stars

STORING

The finished cake can be kept for up to one week in an airtight container.

1 Cut the cake horizontally into three layers. Sandwich the layers together with three-quarters of the butter icing. Spread the remaining butter icing in a thin layer over the top and sides.

2 Colour 500 g/1¼ lb of the sugarpaste icing purple with the grape violet and a touch of the mulberry food colourings. Roll out on a work surface lightly dusted with icing sugar and cover the cake. Leave to dry overnight.

3 ▲ Place the cake on a sheet of greaseproof paper to protect the work surface. Water down a little of the gold and lilac shimmer powdered food colourings, then load up the end of a paintbrush with one of the colours. Position the brush over the area you want to colour, then flick your wrist in the direction of the cake, so the colour falls on to it in small beads. Repeat with the other colour until the whole cake is covered. Leave to dry.

4 To make the stars, divide the remaining sugarpaste icing into three portions. Colour one portion purple, the same as the coated cake, one portion with the lilac shimmer and one portion with the primrose sparkle. Roll out each colour separately to about 3 mm/⅛ inch thick. Cut out stars with the star-shaped cutter and place on a piece of greaseproof paper. You will need 30 stars total. Highlight the stars with the dry powdered colours, brushing gold on the purple stars, primrose on the yellow and lilac on the lilac stars. Using the watered-down gold and lilac colours, flick them on to each star as before.

5 ▲ While the icing is still soft, cut short lengths of florist's wire and carefully push them through the middle of 15 of the stars, but not all the way through. Leave to dry overnight.

6 ▲ Position the cake on the cake board or plate. Arrange three unwired stars in each colour in a diagonal line on the top edge of the cake, securing with a little water. Repeat to make four more groupings of the stars. Stick the wired stars at angles all over the top of the cake as you arrange the flat ones.

7 Decorate the base of the cake with the ribbon.

Marbled Cracker Cake

Here is a Christmas cake decorated in an untraditional way. The cake can be made well ahead of Christmas and then decorated nearer the time.

Ingredients

Serves 20–25

20 cm/8 inch round Rich Fruit Cake
3 tbsp apricot jam, warmed and sieved
675 g/1½ lb marzipan
800 g/1¾ lb/2⅓ x quantity Sugarpaste Icing
red and green food colourings
edible gold balls

Materials and Equipment

wooden cocktail sticks
25 cm/10 inch round cake board
red, green and gold thin gift wrapping ribbon
3 red and 3 green ribbon bows

Storing

The finished cake can be kept for up to three months in an airtight container.

1 Brush the cake with the jam. Roll out the marzipan on a work surface lightly dusted with icing sugar and cover the cake. Leave to dry for 12 hours.

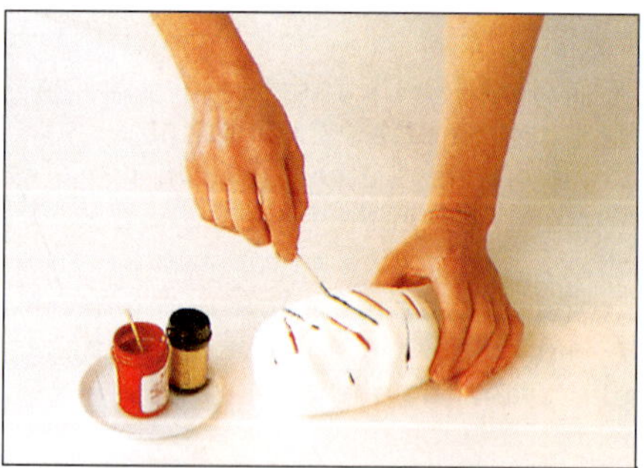

2 ▲ Take 500 g/1¼ lb of the sugarpaste icing and form a smooth roll. Put some red food colouring on the end of a cocktail stick and dab a few drops on to the icing. Repeat with the green. Knead just a few times. Roll out the sugarpaste, on a work surface lightly dusted with icing sugar, until marbled.

3 Brush the marzipan with a little water and cover with the icing. Position the cake on the cake board.

4 ▲ Colour half of the remaining sugarpaste icing red and the rest green. Roll about half of the red icing into five 5 x 1 cm/2 x ½ inch rectangles for the crackers. Roll half of the green icing into a 13 x 1 cm/5 x ½ inch roll and cut off ten 1 cm/½ inch lengths. These are the ends of the crackers. Attach two green ends to each red cracker with a little water. Gather together any icing trimmings. Roll out a small piece of green icing thinly and cut into two 13 x 1 cm/5 x ½ inch strips. Cut each strip into five diamonds. Attach two green diamonds to each cracker, then press a gold ball in the centre. Leave to dry on greaseproof paper for several hours or overnight.

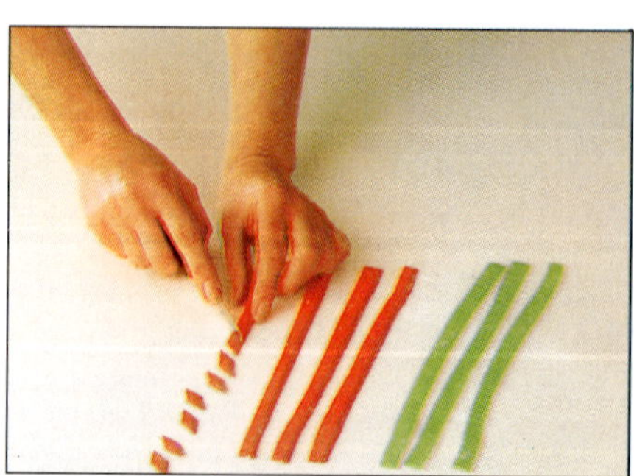

5 ▲ Meanwhile, roll out the remaining red and green icings, including any trimmings, into 1 cm/½ inch wide strips. Cut each strip into diamonds – you will need about 24 diamonds in each colour.

6 ▲ Attach alternate red and green diamonds around the top and base of the cake, securing with water.

7 ▲ Cut the ribbons into about 10 cm/4 inch lengths. Run the blade of a pair of scissors or a sharp knife down the length of them to curl.

8 Arrange the crackers in a pile on top of the cake and decorate with the curled ribbons. Attach the bows in alternate colours with a little softened sugarpaste icing, evenly spaced between the diamonds around the top edge of the cake.

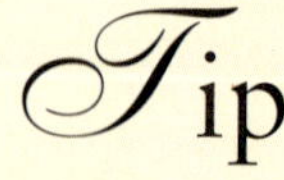

Tip

Add the colour to the icing sparingly at first because the colour becomes more intense as the icing stands. It is advisable to leave the icing for about 10 minutes to see if it is the shade you need.

Trailing Orchid Wedding Cake

A special celebration such as a wedding deserves a very special cake.

Ingredients
Serves 100
30 cm/12 inch round Madeira Cake mix
25 cm/10 inch round Madeira Cake mix
50 g/2 oz/2 squares plain chocolate
50 g/2 oz/2 squares white chocolate
7½ x quantity Butter Icing
1½ x quantity chocolate-flavour Butter Icing

MATERIALS AND EQUIPMENT
30 cm/12 inch oval cake tin
25 cm/10 inch oval cake tin
about 22 rose leaves
plain scraper
several greaseproof paper piping bags
No 4 writing and basket-weave nozzles
35 cm/14 inch oval thick cake board
25 cm/10 inch oval thin cake board
orchids

STORING
Decorate the cake the day before the wedding, adding the leaves and flowers on the day.

1 Grease the oval cake tins, line with a double thickness of greaseproof paper and grease the paper. Make the cakes one at a time and bake, following the baking times for the 30 cm/12 inch and 25 cm/10 inch round Madeira cakes. Leave to cool slightly in the tin, then turn out on to a wire rack, peel off the lining paper and leave to cool.

2 To make the chocolate leaves, wash and dry the rose leaves well on kitchen paper. Melt the chocolates in two separate heatproof bowls over pans of hot water.

3 ▲ Brush the underside of each leaf, some with plain, some with the white chocolate. Do not go over to the other side of the leaf. Place the leaves chocolate-side up on baking parchment, and leave to set in a cool place. Peel the leaf from the chocolate. Handle the chocolate as little as possible as the warmth of your hands will melt it. If the chocolate seems too thin, re-coat.

4 Make the butter icings in batches, whisking until smooth. Level off the tops of the cakes if they have domed. Cut each cake in half horizontally, then sandwich each one back together with some of the plain butter icing.

5 Invert each cake on to a board covered with greaseproof paper. Spread some of the plain butter icing over the sides and smooth with the scraper.

6 ▲ Spread the icing over the top of each cake. To make the surface really smooth, spread with a long metal palette knife which has been dipped into hot water.

7 ▲ To pipe the basket-weave design on each cake, spoon some of the chocolate-flavour butter icing into a greaseproof paper piping bag fitted with a No 4 writing nozzle. (You will need to work in batches with several piping bags.) Pipe a vertical line on the side of the cake from the base to the top of the cake. Pipe several more lines.

8 Spoon some of the plain butter icing into a fresh piping bag fitted with a basket-weave nozzle. (You will need to work in batches with several piping bags.) Across the second vertical line of chocolate icing, pipe 2 cm/¾ inch horizontal lines of basic butter icing, going across the vertical line at 1 cm/½ inch intervals. You will need about three horizontal lines across each vertical for the smaller cake and three to four for the larger one. Fill in the spaces between the horizontal lines with an alternating row of horizontal lines over the third chocolate vertical. Repeat until the sides of each cake have been covered with the design.

9 ▲ Transfer the larger cake to the thick cake board and the smaller cake to the thin one (you should not be able to see the thin board). Keeping the smaller cake on the thin board, position it on top of the larger cake, to one end. Using a piping bag fitted with a No 4 writing nozzle, pipe beads of chocolate butter icing round the top and bottom edges of each cake. Keep in a cool place overnight. On the day, arrange the chocolate leaves and orchids on the tops of each cake. Keep in a cool place until required.

Children's Party Cakes

A special cake is the perfect way to celebrate a child's birthday or other important event. Filled with novelty and fun cake ideas for children of all ages – dinosaurs, monsters, clowns, caterpillars, puppies and many, many more – the cakes in this chapter will make every kid's party an instant success.

Clown Cake

Made from a clown-shaped tin, this is a quick and easy cake to make and decorate. Choose your own nozzle shapes for the designs, following the contours of the cake.

INGREDIENTS
Serves 10–15
1½ x quantity Quick-Mix Sponge Cake mix
115 g/4 oz/⅓ quantity Sugarpaste Icing
2 x quantity Butter Icing
yellow, red, pink and blue food colourings
small coloured sweets, for the features

MATERIALS AND EQUIPMENT
900 g/2 lb clown-shaped cake tin
25 x 30 cm/10 x 12 inch cake board
greaseproof paper piping bags
small star, small plain and large star nozzles
small party hat

STORING
The finished cake can be stored in an airtight container in a cool, dry place for up to two days.

1 ▲ Preheat the oven to 180°C/350°F/Gas 4. Grease the cake tin generously. Spoon in the cake mixture and smooth the surface. Bake in the centre of the oven for 45–50 minutes or until a skewer inserted into the centre of the cake comes out clean. Leave for 5 minutes before turning out on to a wire rack to cool.

2 ▲ To make a template for the clown's face, hold a piece of greaseproof paper firmly over the face on the cooled tin. Draw around the outline using a pencil and cut around the shape.

3 ▲ On a work surface lightly dusted with icing sugar, roll out the sugarpaste icing to about 5 mm/¼ inch thick, then place the greaseproof paper template on top. Use a small sharp knife to cut around the outline of the template. Place the cut-out sugarpaste on a baking sheet and cover with clear film.

4 To colour the butter icing, place about one-third of the icing in a small mixing bowl and colour it yellow. Place another third in another mixing bowl and colour it red. Divide the remaining butter icing between two small bowls and colour one pink and the other blue.

5 ▲ Place the cake on the cake board. Fit a small star nozzle in a paper piping bag and fill it with the yellow butter icing. Use to pipe along the contours of the hair on the clown's head. Place the cut-out sugarpaste template in position on the cake, then place a small plain nozzle in another piping bag and fill with the red butter icing. Use it to pipe decoratively around the neck and torso area of the clown. Pipe around the mouth, then change the nozzle to a large star shape and pipe in the nose.

6 Place a small star nozzle in another small piping bag and fill with the pink icing. Use to pipe a star border around the edges of the sugarpaste template. Place a large star nozzle in another piping bag and fill with the blue icing. Use to pipe in the buttons and the clown's eyes. Place the sweets in the centres of the eyes, nose and buttons. Position the hat.

Nurse's Set

This is a simple cake to make. Any toy medical equipment is suitable to use, but make sure it doesn't get confused with the edible bits!

Ingredients

Serves 12–15

1½ x quantity chocolate-flavour Quick-Mix Sponge Cake mix
8 tbsp apricot jam, warmed and sieved
675 g/1½ lb/2 x quantity Sugarpaste Icing
pink and red food colourings

MATERIALS AND EQUIPMENT

35 x 20 cm/14 x 8 inch roasting tin
25 cm/10 inch square cake board
selection of toy medical equipment

STORING

The finished cake can be kept in a cool, dry place for up to two days.

1 Preheat the oven to 180°C/350°F/Gas 4. Grease the roasting tin, line the base and sides with greaseproof paper and grease the paper. Spoon in the cake mixture and smooth the surface. Bake in the centre of the oven for 45–50 minutes or until a skewer inserted into the centre of the cake comes out clean. Leave the cake in the tin for about 5 minutes, then turn out on to a wire rack, peel off the lining paper and leave to cool completely.

2 ▲ Place the cake, dome side down, and cut in half widthways.

3 ▲Turn one half of the cake dome side up, then use a small, sharp knife to indent a border about 1 cm/½ inch in from the edge and about the same measurement deep, around the three uncut edges. Cut out the centre in strips, keeping the edges neat. Brush the tops and sides of both halves of the cake with the apricot jam.

4 Cut off about 150 g/5 oz of the sugarpaste icing and colour it deep pink. Cut off about 15 g/½ oz from this and shape into a small handle for the box. Carefully wrap in clear film and set aside. Lightly dust the work surface with icing sugar and roll out the remaining pink icing and use to cover the cake board. Trim the edges. Cut off about 15 g/½ oz from the remaining white icing and colour it red. Cover with clear film and set aside. Colour the remaining icing light pink and divide into two portions, one slightly bigger than the other.

5 Roll out the slightly bigger portion of light pink icing and use to cover the base of the nurse's box, gently easing it into the hollow and along the edges. Trim the edges, then position the covered cake on the cake board.

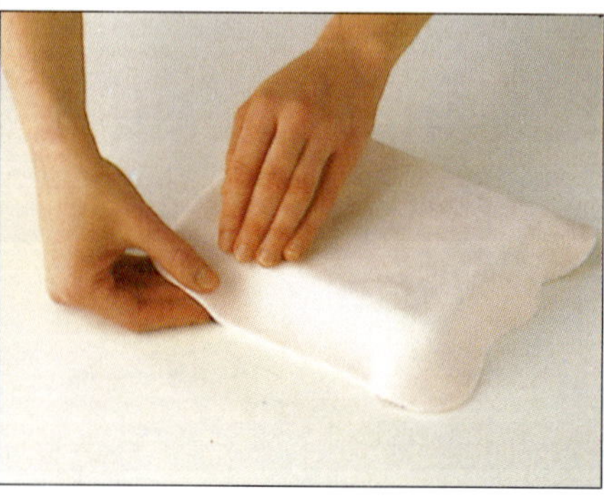

6 ▲ Roll out the other portion of light pink icing and use to cover the lid of the box, using your hands to ease it over the edges. Trim the edges. Place on top of the other cake, back a little and slightly turned to an angle.

7 ▲ Stick the handle on to the bottom section of the box, using a little water. Roll out the red icing and cut out a small cross. Use a little water to stick the cross on the lid of the box. Carefully insert a few toy items into the box, allowing them to hang over the edges a little. Arrange any other items of toy medical equipment around the board and cake when it is positioned on the table.

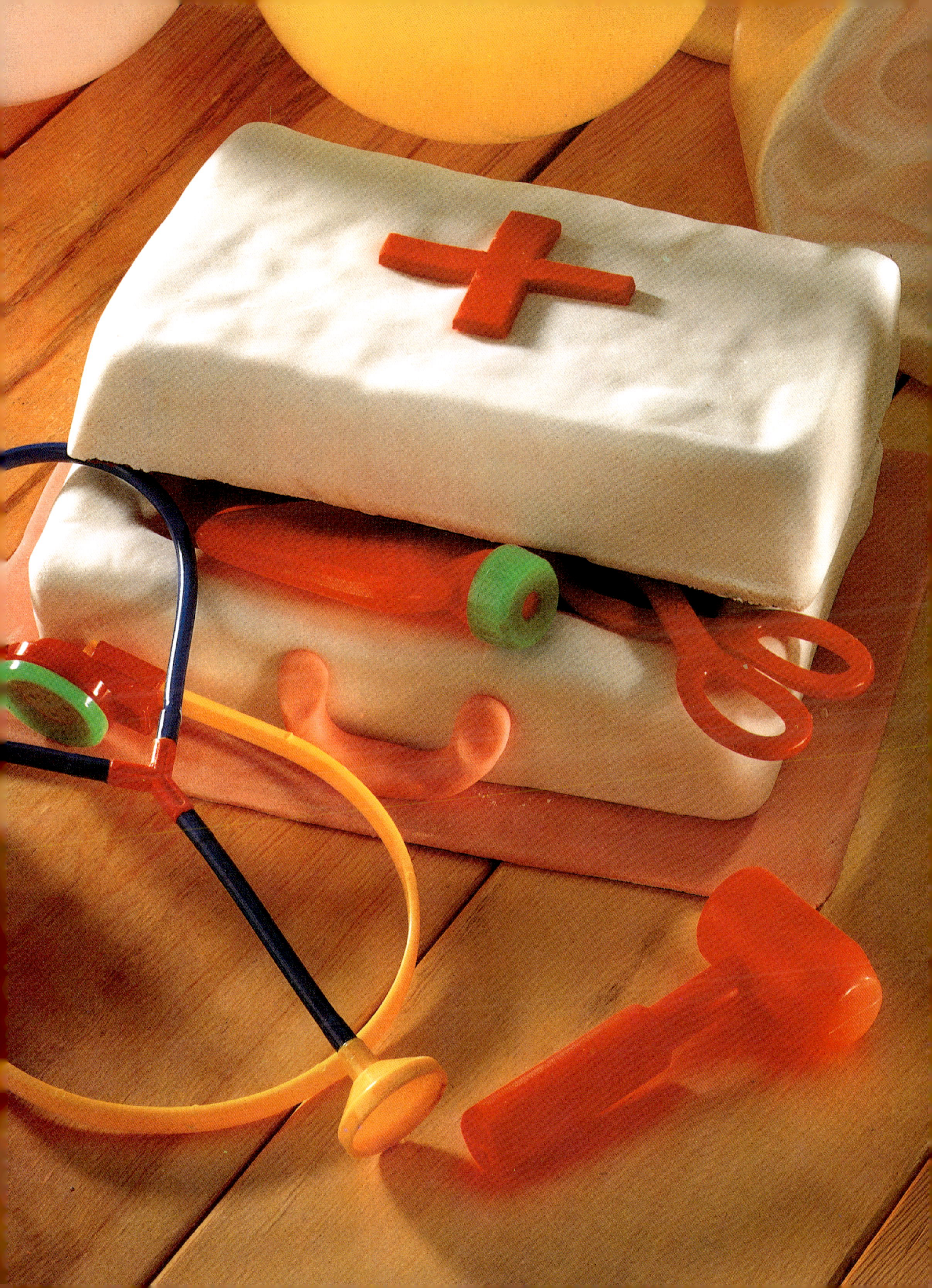

Spiders' Web Cake

A spooky cake for any occasion, fancy dress or otherwise. Put as many spiders as you like on the cake, but any leftover ones can be put on the children's plates or arranged to look like they're crawling all over the table.

INGREDIENTS

Serves 6–8

1 quantity lemon-flavour Quick-Mix Sponge Cake mix
1 quantity lemon-flavour Glacé Icing
yellow and black food colourings

For the Spiders

115 g/4 oz/4 squares plain chocolate, broken into pieces
150 ml/¼ pint/⅔ cup double cream
3 tbsp ground almonds
cocoa powder, for dusting
chocolate vermicelli
2-3 liquorice wheels, sweet centres removed
15 g/½ oz Sugarpaste Icing

MATERIALS AND EQUIPMENT

900 g/2 lb fluted dome-shaped tin or pudding basin
20 cm/8 inch cake board
small greaseproof paper piping bag
wooden skewer

STORING

The finished cake can be kept in a cool, dry place for up to two days.

1 Preheat the oven to 180°C/350°F/ Gas 4. Grease and flour the fluted dome-shaped tin or pudding basin. Spoon in the cake mixture and smooth the surface. Bake in the centre of the oven for 35–40 minutes or until a skewer inserted into the centre of the cake comes out clean.

2 ▲ Leave the cake in the tin for about 5 minutes, then turn out on to a wire rack and leave to cool completely.

3 Place about 3 tbsp of the glacé icing in a small bowl. Stir a few drops of yellow food colouring into the larger quantity of icing and colour the small quantity black. Place the cake on the cake board, dome side up, and pour over the yellow icing, allowing it to run, unevenly, down the sides. Fill the piping bag with the black icing. Seal the bag and snip the end, making a small hole for the nozzle.

4 ▲ Starting on the top of the cake, in the centre, drizzle the black icing round the cake in a spiral, keeping the line as continuous and as evenly spaced as possible. Use the wooden skewer to draw through the icing, downwards from the centre at the top of the cake, to make a web effect. Wipe away the excess icing with a damp cloth, then allow the icing to set at room temperature.

5 To make the spiders, place the chocolate and cream in a small, heavy-based saucepan and heat gently, stirring frequently, until the chocolate melts. Transfer the mixture to a small mixing bowl and allow to cool.

6 ▲ When cool, beat the mixture for about 10 minutes or until thick and pale. Stir in the ground almonds, then chill until firm enough to handle. Dust your hands with a little cocoa, then make a ball the size of a large walnut out of the chocolate mixture. Roll each ball in chocolate vermicelli until evenly coated. Repeat this process until all the mixture is used.

7 ▲ To make the spiders' legs, cut the liquorice into 4 cm/1½ inch lengths. Make small cuts into the sides of each spider, then insert the legs. To make the spiders' eyes, pull off a piece of sugarpaste icing about the size of a hazelnut and colour it with black food colouring. Use the white icing to make tiny balls and the black icing to make even smaller ones. Use a little water to stick the eyes in place. Arrange the spiders on and around the cake.

Puppies in Love

Out of one Swiss roll come two gorgeous puppy dogs. This cake looks extremely impressive, without being too difficult to prepare.

INGREDIENTS
Serves 8–10
1 quantity chocolate-flavour Swiss Roll mix
¼ quantity chocolate-flavour Butter Icing
115 g/4 oz yellow marzipan
green, brown, pink and red food colourings
75 g/3 oz/1½ cups desiccated coconut
450 g/1 lb/1⅓ x quantity Sugarpaste Icing
4 tbsp apricot jam, warmed and sieved

MATERIALS AND EQUIPMENT
33 x 23 cm/13 x 9 inch Swiss roll tin
25 cm/10 inch square cake board
small round cutter
10 cm/4 inch piece of thin ribbon

STORING
The finished cake can be kept in a cool, dry place for up to two days.

1 Preheat the oven to 180°C/350°F/ Gas 4. Grease the Swiss roll tin, line with greaseproof paper and grease the paper. Spoon in the cake mixture and smooth the surface. Bake in the centre of the oven for about 12 minutes or until springy when touched in the centre. Leave to cool in the tin, on a wire rack, covered with a clean, just-damp cloth. Then invert the cake on to a sheet of greaseproof paper, dredged with icing sugar.

2 Trim the edges of the cake, then spread with the chocolate butter icing, reserving a tiny amount. Roll up the Swiss roll, using the greaseproof paper as a guide, then cut in half widthways.

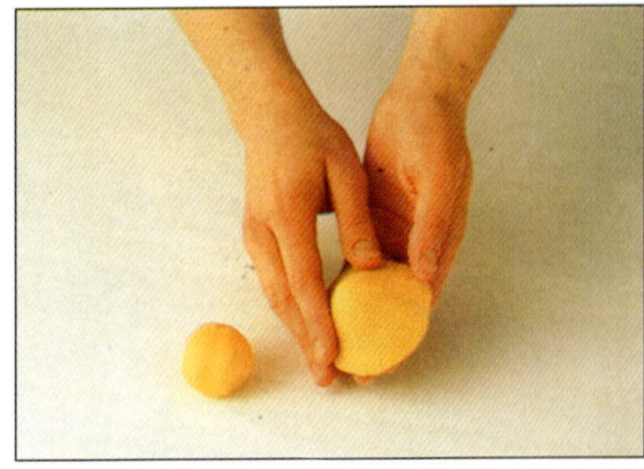

3 ▲ To make the faces, cut the marzipan in half and roll each portion into a ball, then into a squat cone shape. Use a little of the reserved butter icing to stick the faces on to the bodies.

4 Place a few drops of green food colouring in a bowl with the desiccated coconut. Add a few drops of water and stir until the coconut is flecked with green and white. Scatter it over the cake board then position the two puppies a little apart on the board.

5 Cut off about 25 g/1 oz of the sugarpaste icing and set aside, wrapped in clear film. Colour half the remaining icing brown and half pink. Cut off about 50 g/2 oz from each colour and wrap in clear film.

6 ▲ Lightly dust the work surface with icing sugar and roll out the larger portions of brown and pink icings into 11 x 35 cm/4½ x 14 inch rectangles. Cut in half widthways and trim the edges. Cover all four sections with clear film and set aside.

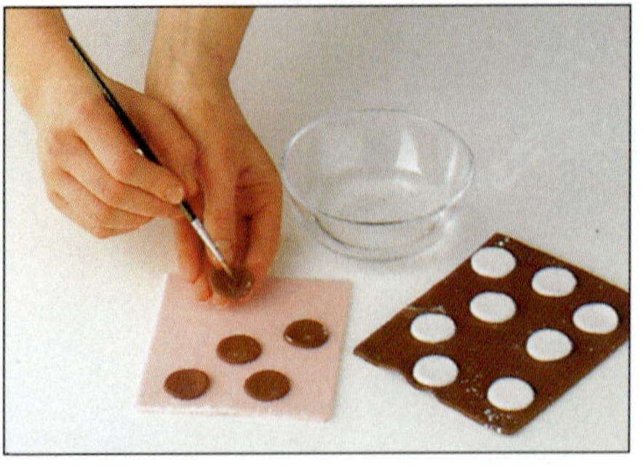

7 ▲ Roll out the reserved pieces of brown and white icings, then use the small round cutter to stamp out several shapes. Gather up the icing trimmings and set aside, wrapped in clear film. Stick the white rounds on to one of the brown rectangles, then the brown rounds on to one of the pink rectangles, using a little water. Use a rolling pin to press them in slightly.

8 Use a sharp knife to slash all four icing rectangles along the two short edges. Brush the body of each puppy with jam, then lay the brown icing without spots over one body, and the pink icing without spots over the other. Place a little water on the back of each, then put the brown spotty icing over the brown dog and the pink spotty icing over the pink dog.

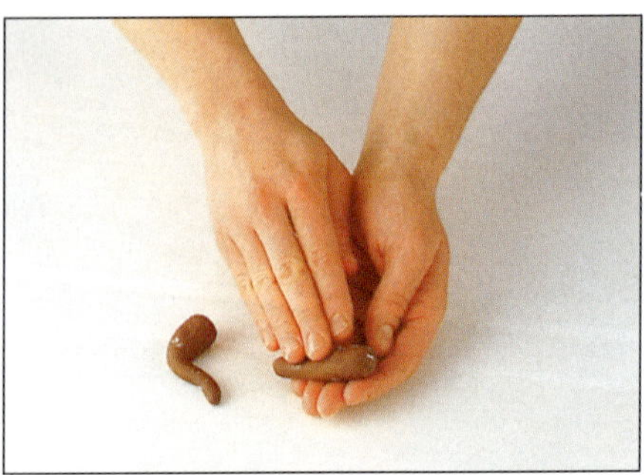

9 ▲ Roll half of the reserved icings in your hands to make little tails. Stick them in place with a little reserved butter icing. Make a little fringe from the brown icing for the brown puppy, and tie a few strands of pink icing together with the ribbon to make a fringe for the pink puppy. Stick them in place with a little water.

10 Use the remaining pieces of sugarpaste icing to make the facial features for each puppy, choosing your own expressions, then stick them in place with some water. The little heart-shaped food bowl is an optional extra, or you can make a small bone, if you prefer.

Crazy Caterpillar

A no-bake cake made from sponge cake crumbs, home-made or bought. You can double the quantity for an extra-large party, but remember the cake is rich and heavy in texture so you only serve a small amount. One ball per person is more than enough!

INGREDIENTS
Serves 11
1 quantity Truffle Cake mix
675 g/1½ lb yellow marzipan
green, brown and orange food colourings
selection of coloured liquorice sticks, or sweets, for the feet
green-coloured desiccated coconut (see Puppies in Love, step 4), for the grass
small flowers, to decorate (optional)

MATERIALS AND EQUIPMENT
40 x 20 cm/16 x 8 inch cake board (optional)
small round fluted cutter
round fluted aspic cutter

STORING
The finished cake can be wrapped in clear film and kept in a cool, dry place for up to four days.

1 ▲ Using slightly damp hands, roll the truffle cake mixture into balls about the size of a large walnut. Place them on a baking sheet as you make them, then cover with clear film and set to one side.

2 ▲ Divide the marzipan into three equal portions, then colour one portion green, one portion brown and the other portion orange. Remove a small amount of orange and green marzipan, to make the face features, and set aside, covered with clear film.

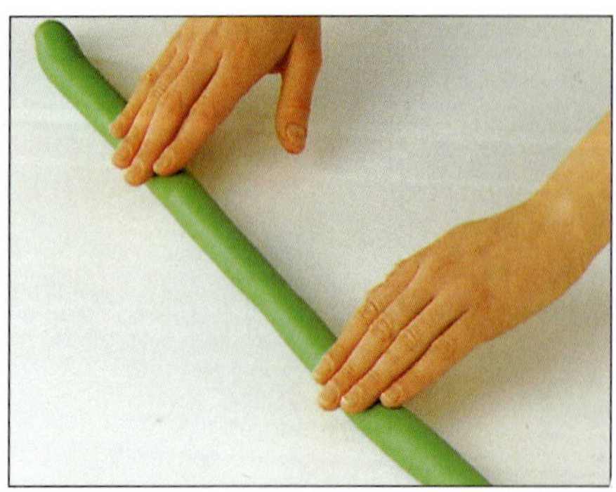

3 ▲ Roll each colour of marzipan into a sausage shape about 45 cm/18 inches long on a work surface lightly dusted with icing sugar. Make sure the sausage shape is even all the way along; if it breaks, compress the marzipan into a ball and start again.

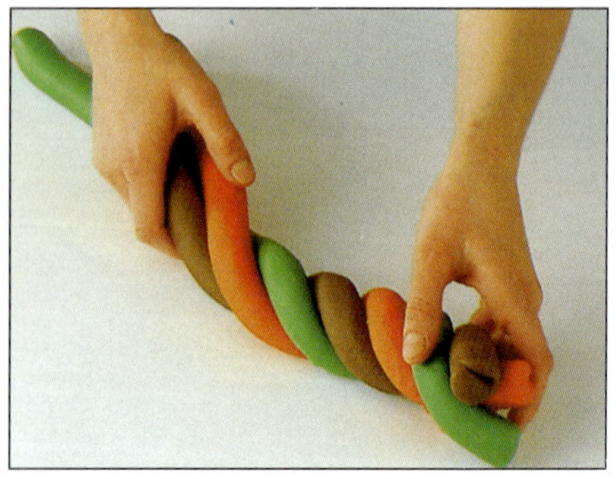

4 ▲ Place the three long sausages side-by-side on the work surface. Starting at one end, hold them together firmly and start to turn them in a twisting motion — do not squeeze. Place the twist back on the work surface, then use a rolling pin to push and roll the twist gently until it is flat and the colours merge. It should be about 50 cm/20 inches long.

5 Lay the truffle balls all along the length of the marzipan strip, then wrap the marzipan evenly around the balls, sealing the join by pinching the marzipan together. (An extra pair of hands is useful for this stage.) Turn the caterpillar over so the join is underneath, tucking in and cutting off any excess marzipan from the ends. Lift the caterpillar on to the cake board, if using, otherwise position it on the table, curving it slightly.

6 Roll out the reserved orange and green marzipan thinly and use the fluted cutters to stamp out rounds for the eyes. Use a little water to stick the smaller green rounds on the orange rounds, then stick them on to one end of the caterpillar to make the face. Roll a tiny piece of orange marzipan into a little sausage, shape and stick it on to make the mouth. Cut the liquorice sticks into small pieces and position them along either side, to make the feet. Scatter the green-coloured coconut all around. Add a few flowers, if you like.

Elephant Cake

Any medium-sized roasting tin will work for this cake, but one with rounded edges is preferable as this improves the finished result.

Ingredients

Serves 10–12

1½ x quantity lemon-flavour Quick-Mix Sponge Cake mix
1 quantity lemon-flavour Butter Icing (optional)
8 tbsp apricot jam, warmed and sieved
900 g/2 lb/2⅔ x quantity Sugarpaste Icing
pink, blue and grey food colourings

MATERIALS AND EQUIPMENT

30 x 23 cm/12 x 9 inch roasting tin
18 cm/7 inch round cake tin, or card, to use as a template
40 cm/16 inch round cake board, with a support for the trunk, or 40 x 25 cm/16 x 10 inch square cake board (optional)
wooden cocktail stick
medium-size round cutter (optional)
bow made from pretty ribbon
pin

STORING

The finished cake can be kept in a cool, dry place for up to two days.

1 Preheat the oven to 180°C/350°F/Gas 4. Grease the roasting tin, line the base and sides with greaseproof paper and grease the paper. Spoon in the cake mixture and smooth the surface. Bake in the centre of the oven for 45–50 minutes or until a skewer inserted into the centre of the cake comes out clean. Leave in the tin for about 5 minutes, then turn out on to a wire rack, peel off the lining paper and leave to cool completely.

2 ▲ Place the cake, dome side down, on the work surface and position the template in the centre on the flat surface. Use a sharp knife to cut around the template, holding it steady and firm as you cut. Lift out the cut-out circle, keeping the outside piece intact.

3 ▲ Use the template to cut out the elephant's trunk. Place the template close to one edge of the short side of the remaining cake and cut out a crescent shape. Cut off one end of the crescent to make the elephant's mouth. Cut off the other end of the cake, just past the rounded corners, to make the ear. Discard the two small, middle sections of cake. Cut horizontally through the face, ear, trunk and mouth sections of the cake, then sandwich them back together with lemon butter icing, if you are using it.

4 ▲ Assemble the cake on a board or directly on the table. Place the ear piece on one side of the round face, then place the flat edge of the trunk section up against the face, opposite the ear. Place the mouth section in the space between the trunk and the face. Brush the whole surface with jam.

5 Cut off about 50 g/2 oz of sugarpaste icing and set aside, wrapped in clear film. Cut off another 175 g/6 oz of sugarpaste icing and colour it pink, and 15 g/½ oz and colour it blue. Set aside, wrapped in clear film. Colour the remaining icing grey, cut off about 75 g/3 oz and set aside. Dust the work surface with icing sugar then roll out the larger portion of grey icing into a 50 x 25 cm/20 x 10 inch rectangle. Use this to cover the entire cake. Smooth down the sides and edges, snipping with scissors or cutting the icing in the places where it overlaps. Trim the edges.

6 To make the ear piece, roll out the reserved portion of grey icing into a 20 x 10 cm/8 x 4 inch rectangle, then roll it in small sections with the cocktail stick, to give a ruffled effect (see Teddy Bear Christening cake, step 7). Lay this section on top of the ear, slightly off centre. Cut off about 150 g/5 oz of the pink icing and roll it out to a slightly smaller rectangle, then repeat the ruffling process with the cocktail stick. Lay this piece on top of the grey ruffle.

7 Roll out the reserved blue and white icings and cut out the eye parts, using the round cutter, if preferred. Stick in place with a little water, placing a small round ball of the remaining pink icing in the centre. Roll out the remaining pink icing and cut out a triangular piece for the mouth. Shape the remaining white icing into a tusk and then stick them both in place with a little water. Finally, position the bow, securing in place with the pin, which must be removed before serving the cake.

The Beehive

The perfect cake for an outdoors spring or summer party. Take the bees along separately on their wires and insert them into the cake at the picnic.

INGREDIENTS
Serves 8–10
1 quantity Quick-Mix Sponge Cake mix
900 g/2 lb yellow marzipan
5 tbsp apricot jam, warmed and sieved
black food colouring
25 g/1 oz sugarpaste icing

MATERIALS AND EQUIPMENT
900 g/2 lb pudding basin
23 cm/9 inch fluted or round cake board
20 cm/8 inch square of rice paper
florist's wire covered in florist's tape

STORING
The finished cake can be kept in a cool, dry place for up to two days.

1 Preheat the oven to 180°C/350°F/ Gas 4. Grease and flour the pudding basin. Spoon in the cake mixture and smooth the surface. Bake in the centre of the oven for 40–45 minutes or until a skewer inserted into the centre of the cake comes out clean. Leave the cake in the basin for about 5 minutes, then turn out on to a wire rack and leave to cool completely.

2 Cut off about 175 g/6 oz of marzipan and set aside, wrapped in clear film. Knead the remainder on a work surface lightly dusted with icing sugar, then roll it out into a long, thin sausage shape. If it breaks when it gets too long, make more than one sausage. Place the cake, dome side up, on the cake board and brush evenly with apricot jam.

3 ▲ Starting at the back of the base, coil the marzipan sausage around the cake, keeping it neat and tight all the way to the top. Any joins that have to be made should be placed at the back of the cake.

4 ▲ Using a small, sharp knife, cut an arched doorway at the front of the cake. Remove the cut-out section and cut away some of the inside cake to make a hollow. Brush the crumbs away from the doorway.

5 ▲ To make six bees, divide the reserved marzipan in half and colour one portion black. Set aside a cherry-sized ball of black marzipan, and wrap in clear film. Divide both the black and the yellow marzipan into 12 small balls. To make a bee, pinch together two balls of each colour, alternately placed. Stick them together with a little water, if necessary. Cut the rice paper into six pairs of rounded wings, then stick them to the bees with a tiny drop of water.

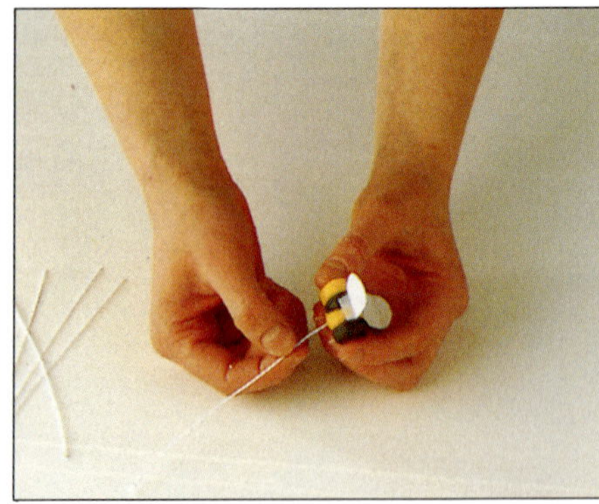

6 ▲ Use the reserved black marzipan and sugarpaste icing to make the facial features. Then cut the florist's wire into various lengths and then use it to pierce the bees from underneath. Once secure, press the other end of the wire into the cake in various places. The wires must be removed before serving.

Strawberry Cake

A summer-time cake or for someone who's simply mad about strawberries!

INGREDIENTS
Serves 10–12
1 quantity Quick-Mix Sponge Cake mix
650 g/1 lb 7oz marzipan
green, red and yellow food colourings
caster sugar, to dredge

MATERIALS AND EQUIPMENT
900 g/2 lb heart-shaped tin
30 cm/12 inch round cake board
icing smoother

STORING
The finished cake can be kept in a cool, dry place for up to two days.

Tip

You can also sandwich the cake with a half quantity of strawberry-flavour Butter Icing before brushing it with apricot jam for extra flavour! Use a long, serrated knife and cut the cake horizontally into two layers.

1 Preheat the oven to 180°C/350°F/ Gas 4. Grease the heart-shaped tin, line the base with greaseproof paper and grease the paper. Spoon in the cake mixture and smooth the surface. Bake in the centre of the oven for 35–40 minutes or until a skewer inserted into the centre of the cake comes out clean.

2 Leave in the tin for about 5 minutes, then turn out on to a wire rack, peel off the lining paper and leave to cool completely.

3 ▲ Cut off about 175 g/6 oz of the marzipan and colour it green. Brush the cake board with a little apricot jam, then roll out the green marzipan on the work surface lightly dusted with icing sugar and use to cover the cake board. Trim the edges. Use an icing smoother to make the marzipan as flat and as smooth as possible.

4 ▲ Evenly brush the remaining apricot jam over the top and sides of the cake. Position the cake on the cake board. Cut off about 275 g/10 oz of the remaining marzipan and colour it red. Roll it out to about 5 mm/¼ inch thick and use to cover the cake, smoothing down the sides and edges. Trim the edges. Use the handle of a teaspoon to indent the strawberry evenly and lightly all over.

5 To make the stalk, cut off another 175 g/6 oz of marzipan and colour it bright green. Cut it in half and roll out one portion into a 10 x 15 cm/4 x 6 inch rectangle. Use a sharp knife to cut 'V' shapes out of the rectangle, leaving a 2.5 cm/1 inch border across the top, to form the calyx. Position this on the cake, curling and moving the sections to make them look more realistic.

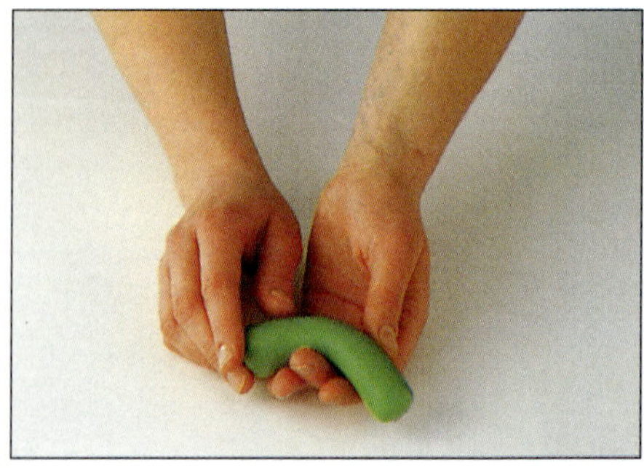

6 ▲ Roll the other half of the green marzipan in your hands into a sausage shape about 13 cm/5 inches long. Bend it slightly, then position it on the cake to form the stalk.

7 ▲ To make the strawberry seeds, colour the remaining marzipan yellow. Pull off tiny pieces about the size of an apple pip and roll them into little tear-shaped seeds. Place them in the indentations all over the strawberry. Dust the cake and board with sifted caster sugar.

Daisy Cow

A really fun cake to make for a child who loves animals or the countryside.

INGREDIENTS

Serves 10–12

1½ x quantity Quick-Mix Sponge Cake mix
9 tbsp apricot jam, warmed and sieved
1.67 kg/3 lb 12 oz/5 x quantity Sugarpaste Icing
black, brown, blue, yellow and red food colourings

MATERIALS AND EQUIPMENT

2 x deep 18 cm/7 inch round cake tins
25 x 33 cm/10 x 13 inch cake board
4 cm/1½ inch and 2.5 cm/1 inch plain round pastry cutters
6 cm/2½ inch fluted round pastry cutter
wooden cocktail stick
25 cm/10 inch florist's wire covered in florist's tape

STORING

The finished cake can be kept in a cool, dry place for up to three days.

1 Preheat the oven to 180°C/350°F/ Gas 4. Grease the tins, line the bases with greaseproof paper and grease the paper. Divide the cake mixture equally between the two tins and smooth the surfaces. Bake in the centre of the oven for 30–35 minutes or until a skewer inserted into the centre of each cake comes out clean. Turn out on to wire racks, peel off the lining paper and leave to cool completely.

2 ▲ Using a sharp, pointed knife, cut a crescent-shaped piece from the side of one cake, then cut it in half to make the cow's ears.

3 ▲ This is how the cake should be assembled. On the work surface, brush the cake with apricot jam and push the two rounds together to make the face.

4 Colour 950 g/2 lb 2 oz of the sugarpaste icing with black food colouring. Cut off 500 g/1 lb 2 oz and set aside, wrapped in clear film. Roll out the remainder on a work surface dusted with icing sugar into a rectangle about 5 mm/¼ inch thick. Roll out two-thirds of the white icing, then cut into rounds using plain round cutters. Place some of the rounds of white icing in a random pattern on the rolled-out black icing and roll again lightly with the rolling pin to flatten them into the surface. Cover the cow's face with the black and white icing, trimming it neatly around the bottom edge. Brush the cake board evenly with apricot jam. Roll out 275 g/10 oz of the reserved black icing into an oblong large enough to cover the cake board.

5 Arrange the circles of white icing on top of the black icing and roll lightly into the surface. Lay over the cake board and trim the edges. Set aside 50 g/2 oz of the black icing, break off two marble-size pieces and set aside from the rest for the cow's eyes. Roll out the icing that is left and use to cover the ear shapes.

6 Carefully lift the cow's head on to the cake board, set aside 90 g/3½ oz of the white icing then roll out the rest thinly. Cut out a pear shape for the cow's nose. Brush the back with a little water and stick on to the cake. Roll two small pieces of white icing into walnut-size balls, then flatten with a rolling pin and reserve for the eyes.

7 To make the cow's eyes, colour 40 g/1½ oz sugarpaste icing brown, then cut out two rounds with the 4 cm/1½ inch round pastry cutter. Colour 25 g/1 oz icing blue, then cut out two rounds with the 2.5 cm/1 inch round cutter. Assemble the cow's eyes from the brown and blue rounds and the reserved white and black icings. Stick them in place with a little water.

8 Divide the reserved 50 g/2 oz of the black sugarpaste icing in half, and roll out one half thinly into a rectangle of about 15 x 10 cm/6 x 4 inches. Cut along the icing at intervals, leaving a 1 cm /½ inch border along the top, to create the fringe. Position between the ears. Divide the remaining sugarpaste icing in half and use for the nose.

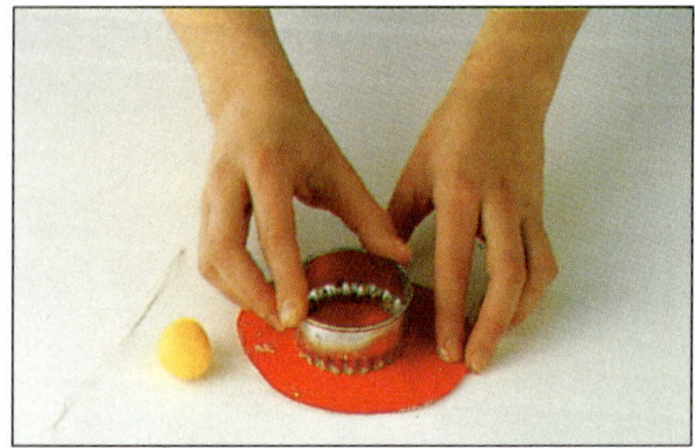

9 ▲ Colour 25 g/1 oz of the remaining icing bright yellow and the rest red. Roll two-thirds of the red icing into a sausage shape, to make a mouth. To make the flower, roll out the remaining red icing and cut out a 6 cm/2½ inch round, using the fluted cutter.

10 Roll the edge of the red icing using a cocktail stick to make it frilly (see Teddy Bear Christening Cake, step 7). Roll the yellow icing into a ball to finish off the flower. Push the florist's wire through the cake. Remove before serving.

Monsters on the Moon

A great cake for little monsters!
This cake is best eaten on the day of making.

Ingredients

Serves 12–15
1 quantity Quick-Mix Sponge Cake mix
115 g/4 oz/1/3 quantity Sugarpaste Icing
edible silver glitter powder (optional)

For the Icing
375 g/12 oz/1 3/4 cups plus 2 tbsp caster sugar
2 size 3 egg whites
4 tbsp water

MATERIALS AND EQUIPMENT
ovenproof wok
various sizes of plain round cutters
30 cm/12 inch round cake board
several small monster toys

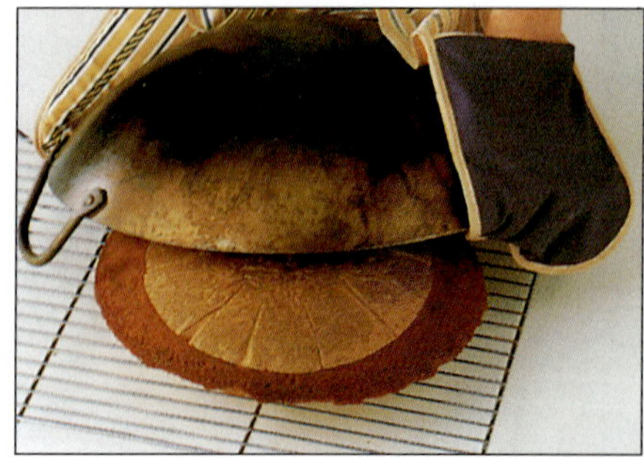

1 ▲ Preheat the oven to 180°C/350°F/ Gas 4. Grease the wok, line the base with greaseproof paper and grease the paper. Spoon in the cake mixture and smooth the surface. Bake in the centre of the oven for 35–40 minutes or until a skewer inserted into the centre of the cake comes out clean. Leave the cake in the wok for about 5 minutes, then turn out on to a wire rack, peel off the lining paper and leave to cool completely.

2 ▲ With the cake dome side up, use the round cutters to cut out craters. Press in a cutter about 2.5 cm/1 inch deep, then remove and use a knife to cut out the cake to make a crater.

3 ▲ Pull off small pieces of the sugarpaste icing and press them into uneven strips which can be moulded around the edges of the craters. Make one of the craters especially deep by adding an extra-wide sugarpaste strip to make the edges higher.

4 Place the cake on the cake board. To make the icing, place all the ingredients in a heatproof bowl, then sit the bowl over a saucepan of simmering water. Beat until thick and peaky. Spoon the icing over the cake, swirling it into the craters and peaking it unevenly. Sprinkle over the silver glitter powder, if using, then position the monsters on the cake.

Tip

To cover the cake board, roll out 450 g/1 lb of black sugarpaste icing. Trim the edges. Using various sizes of star-shaped cutters, stamp out stars from the black icing. Roll out 285 g/8 oz of yellow marzipan thinly and use the star-shaped cutters to stamp out replacement stars. Dust with a little extra silver powder.

Ice-cream Cornets

Individual cakes make a change for a party, the idea being that each guest has one to themselves. You could even put a candle in the special person's one.

INGREDIENTS
Makes 9
1 quantity Quick-Mix Sponge Cake mix
9 ice-cream cornets
1 quantity Butter Icing
red, green and brown food colourings
selection of coloured vermicelli, wafers, chocolate sticks, etc.

MATERIALS AND EQUIPMENT
9 fairy cake paper cases
bun tin

STORING
The finished cakes can be kept in a cool, dry place for up to a day.

Tip

To have 3 sets of 3 ice cream cakes placed on the table, you will need 3 egg boxes, which hold 12 eggs each. Place a ball of marzipan in 3 evenly spaced holes in the upturned egg box. Cover the box in foil, then pierce the foil and make a small hole with your finger where the marzipan balls are. Insert the iced ice cream cornets, pressing them in gently, so they stand securely.

1 Preheat the oven to 180°C/350°F/ Gas 4. Place the paper cases in the bun tin, then spoon in the cake mixture until they are all at least half full. Bake in the centre of the oven for about 20 minutes or until the cakes have risen and are golden. Transfer the cakes to a wire rack to cool completely. Remove the cases.

2 ▲ Gently press a fairy cake into a cornet, taking care not to damage the cornet. If the bases of the cakes are a little large to insert into the cornets, trim them down with a small, sharp knife. The cakes should feel quite secure once inserted into the cornets.

3 Divide the butter icing into three small bowls and colour one portion pale red, one portion green and one portion brown.

4 ▲ Using a small palette knife, spread each cake with some of one of the icings. Place in the ice-cream stand (see Tip). Continue coating the cornets, making sure the icing isn't too smooth so it looks like ice cream.

5 ▲ To insert a wafer or chocolate stick into an ice cream, use a small, sharp knife to make a hole or incision through the icing and into the cake, then insert the wafer or stick. Add the finishing touches by sprinkling over some coloured vermicelli.

Magic Carpet Cake

The Master of the Lamp can also be made out of coloured sugarpaste icing, instead of marzipan, if you prefer.

INGREDIENTS
Serves 8–10
1 quantity Quick-Mix Sponge Cake mix
675 g/1½ lb/2 x quantity Sugarpaste Icing
blue, brown, red, orange, yellow, purple and black food colourings
115 g/4 oz/4 squares milk or plain chocolate, melted
350 g/12 oz white marzipan
small sweet or diamond-shaped cake decoration
small brightly coloured feather

MATERIALS AND EQUIPMENT
23 x 15 cm/6 x 9 inch cake tin
33 cm/13 inch round cake board
2.5 cm/1 inch and 6 cm/2½ inch round fluted pastry cutters
small piece of yellow crepe paper

STORING
The finished cake can be kept in a cool, dry place for up to three days.

1 Preheat the oven to 180°C/350°F/Gas 4. Grease the cake tin, line the base and sides with greaseproof paper and grease the paper. Spoon in the cake mixture and smooth the surface. Bake in the centre of the oven for 30–35 minutes or until a skewer inserted into the centre of the cake comes out clean. Turn out on to a wire rack, peel off the lining paper and leave to cool completely.

2 Colour 275 g/10 oz sugarpaste icing with blue food colouring. Remove a piece about the size of a walnut and set aside, wrapped in clear film. Roll out the rest of the blue icing thinly on a surface dusted with icing sugar into a round about the same size as the cake board.

3 ▲ Roll out about 150 g/5 oz of white icing and cut out rounds using the pastry cutters. Arrange these on the blue icing to resemble clouds, then roll lightly into the icing. Brush the cake board lightly with water and cover with the blue and white icing, smoothing it with your hands to exclude air bubbles. Leave the icing draped over the edge of the board, if liked, or trim level with the edge of the board.

4 ▲ Colour 175 g/6 oz sugarpaste icing dark brown, then roll it out thinly into an oblong large enough to cover the top and sides of the cake generously. Trim the edges. Knead the trimmings into a ball and set aside, wrapped in clear film. Brush the cake with melted chocolate, then place on the cake board. Drape the brown icing over the top of the cake, being careful not to flatten it at the sides too much.

5 Divide 75 g/3 oz sugarpaste icing into two equal pieces. Colour one piece red and the other orange. Then unwrap the reserved pieces of blue and brown icing.

6 Divide each of the four colours into three or four smaller pieces, then knead them together to make a marbled ball of icing. Roll it out into a rectangle slightly larger than the top of the cake. Trim the edges, then lay over the brown icing and stick into place with water.

7 ▲ Colour 75 g/3 oz marzipan yellow, then roll most of it into a long, thin sausage shape. Press it around the edge of the carpet to make a trim. Decorate with small balls of yellow marzipan. Snip pieces of yellow crepe paper with scissors to make tassels. Push into the small balls of icing.

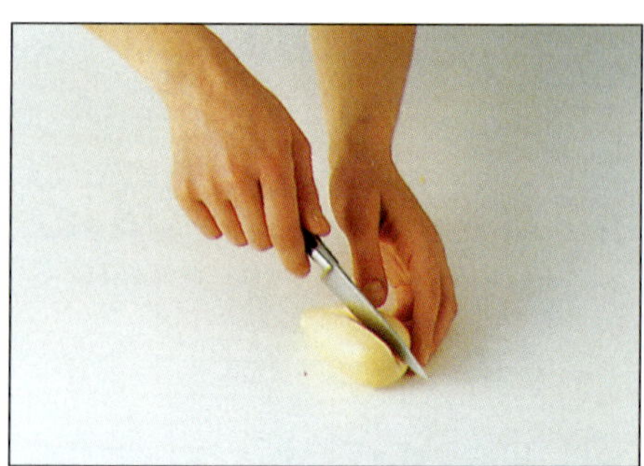

8 ▲ To make the figure, roll about 75 g/3 oz of white marzipan into a pear shape, then cut in half to make two legs. Bend the legs into a sitting position. Colour 65 g/2½ oz marzipan dark brown and shape into a head, body and arms. Make the eyes and mouth from tiny pieces of coloured icing or marzipan and press on to the face. Press the head and body on to the legs. Colour 25 g/1 oz of marzipan purple and use it to make the jacket. Press the arms on to the figure.

9 Colour small pieces of marzipan black and deep red or purple and use to make hair and a hat respectively. Colour the remaining marzipan bright orange. Roll a tiny piece into a ball and press on to the hat. Decorate with a tiny diamond-shaped sweet or cake decoration and coloured feather. Use the rest of the orange marzipan to make slippers and a lamp. Position the figure and the lamp on the carpet.

An Apple Tree

For this unusual centrepiece, choose whichever fruit you prefer. You could make the apples green instead of red, or have a mixture of red and green apples or golden pears.

INGREDIENTS

Serves 10–12

1 quantity chocolate-flavour Quick-Mix Sponge Cake mix
1 quantity chocolate-flavour Swiss Roll, baked and rolled with ¼ quantity chocolate-flavour Butter Icing
¼ quantity chocolate-flavour Butter Icing
½ quantity Butter Icing, coloured green with food colouring
225 g/8 oz marzipan
red and green food colouring
green-coloured desiccated coconut (see Puppies in Love, step 4)
tiny fresh flowers, to decorate (optional)

MATERIALS AND EQUIPMENT

450 g/1 lb fluted round cake tin or pudding basin
15cm/6 inch round cake board
wooden cocktail stick
2 x 30 cm/12 inch lengths of florist's wire
florist's tape
greaseproof paper piping bag
leaf nozzle

STORING

The finished cake can be kept in a cool, dry place for up to a day.

Tip

To stand the tree up at a slight angle, you can cut out a template of thick card from around the un-iced cake. Then decorate the cake on the card and prop it up on a small block of wood. Alternatively, decorate the cake flat on a cake board.

1 Preheat the oven to 180°F/350°C/ Gas 4. Grease and flour the tin or pudding basin. Spoon in the cake mixture and smooth the surface. Bake in the centre of the oven for 35–40 minutes or until a skewer inserted into the centre of the cake comes out clean. Leave in the tin for about 5 minutes, then turn out on to a wire rack and leave to cool.

2 ▲ Arrange the Swiss roll on the card template or cake board (see Tip), trimming it, if necessary. Spread the chocolate butter icing over the tree trunk, making swirls. Use about three-quarters of the green butter icing for the top of the tree, making it peak and swirl. Position on top of the tree trunk.

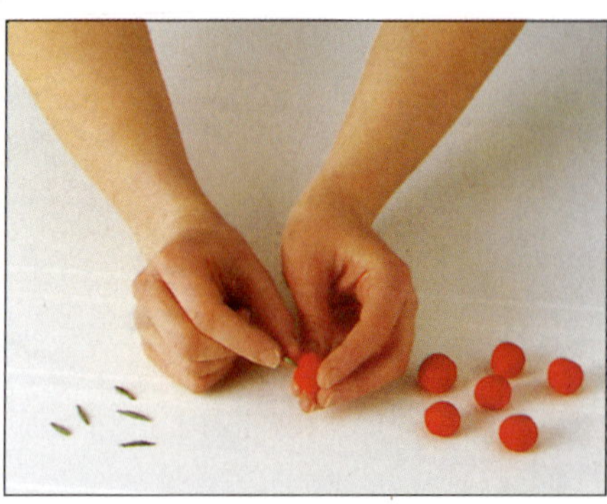

3 ▲ Colour about 25 g/1 oz of the marzipan green. Colour the remainder red, then roll it into cherry-size balls. Roll the green marzipan into tiny sausage shapes to make the stalks and leaves. Use the cocktail stick to make tiny holes in the tops of the apples, then insert the stalks and leaves.

4 ▲ Twist the florist's tape around the florist's wire, then cut it into 7.5 cm/3 inch lengths. Press the lengths of wire through the apples, bending the ends so the apples cannot fall off when hanging. Press the hanging apples into the tree, reserving the extra apples to scatter around the bottom.

5 ▲ Use the remaining green butter icing to fill the piping bag. Practise piping the leaves on a piece of greaseproof paper before piping leaves all over the tree top. Scatter the green desiccated coconut around the base of the tree and pipe a few extra leaves. Add a few tiny fresh flowers for effect, if liked. The wires must be removed from the cake before serving.

Dinosaur Cake

For a dino-crazy kid, this cake is just the ticket. Put it on a cake board or build a little scene using bits and pieces from around the house and garden.

INGREDIENTS
Serves 8–10
1 quantity Quick-Mix Sponge Cake mix
½ quantity Butter Icing
1 quantity Truffle Cake mix
900 g/2 lb/2⅔ x quantity Sugarpaste Icing
pink, yellow, green and black food colourings
4 tbsp apricot jam, warmed and sieved

MATERIALS AND EQUIPMENT
900 g/2 lb heart-shaped tin
5 x 25 cm/2 x 10 inch piece of card
small block of wood, for raising the cake

STORING
The finished cake can be kept in a cool, dry place for up to two days.

1 Preheat the oven to 180°C/350°F/ Gas 4. Grease the heart-shaped tin, line the base with greaseproof paper and grease the paper. Spoon in the cake mixture and smooth the surface. Bake in the centre of the oven for 35–40 minutes or until a skewer inserted into the centre of the cake comes out clean. Turn out on to a wire rack, peel off the lining paper and leave to cool completely.

2 ▲ Cut the heart-shaped cake in half vertically, then sandwich the halves together with the butter icing so they form a half heart shape. Place the cake in the centre of the strip of card, positioned on the long, straight side. Stand the cake on the small block of wood to raise it up slightly.

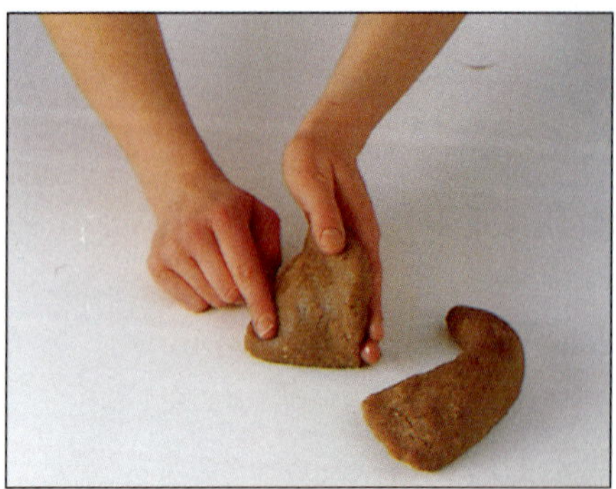

3 ▲ Divide the truffle mixture in half. Shape one portion into the tail, making it thicker and flattened at one end and more pointed at the other. This will fit on the pointed end of the cake. Mould the other half of the truffle cake mix into the head shape, starting with a ball and then flattening one side, so the diameter matches the width of the head end of the cake. Mould the other end of the head into a pointed shape for the nose.

4 Place the head and tail in position at either end of the cake, moulding the truffle cake mix on to the cake a little. Cut off about 500 g/ 1¼ lb of the sugarpaste icing and colour it pink. Lightly dust the work surface with icing sugar and roll out the icing to a long, thin, rectangular shape. Brush the cake evenly with jam and cover the dinosaur with the icing in one piece from head to toe. Smooth down the sides and edges with your hands, then trim.

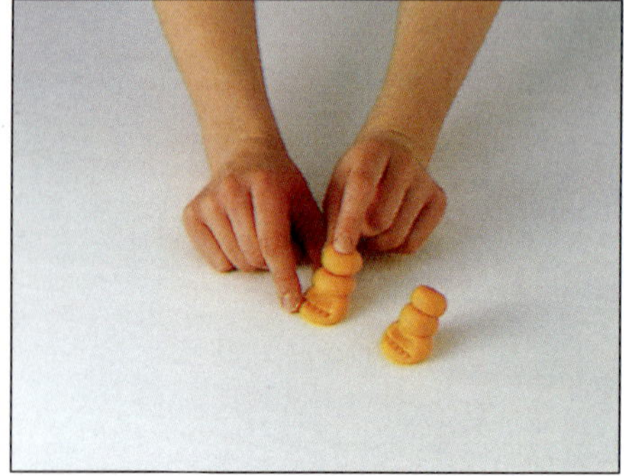

5 ▲ To make the dinosaur's legs, cut off about 115 g/4 oz of the remaining sugarpaste icing and colour it yellow. Remove about 25 g/1 oz and set aside, wrapped in clear film. Use the remainder to roll out 10 evenly sized balls, each about the size of a small walnut. Squeeze together two balls for each of the back legs and three for each of the front ones. Indent the toes with a fork, then using a little water stick the legs on the dinosaur.

6 ▲ Use the reserved yellow sugarpaste icing to make one small and three large horns, then stick these in place with a little water. Cut off about 75 g/3 oz of the remaining icing and colour it green. Divide it into about 11 evenly sized pieces and shape each into a cone. Stick these on to the dinosaur with a little water. Divide the remaining icing in half and colour one portion black. Use the white and black icings to make the mouth, eyes and eyebrows for the dinosaur. Stick on with a little water.

Personal Stereo

This loud cake in noisy colours will be a smash hit! The cake board is optional.

INGREDIENTS
Serves 4–6
1 quantity chocolate-flavour Quick-Mix Sponge Cake mix
¼ quantity chocolate-flavour Butter Icing
4 tbsp apricot jam, warmed and sieved
350 g/12 oz/1 quantity Sugarpaste Icing
orange, green, purple and black food colourings
3 sweets, for the buttons
2 liquorice sweets, for the cassette holes
2 long liquorice bootlaces
2 liquorice wheels

EQUIPMENT AND MATERIALS
20 x13 cm/8 x 5 inch shallow cake tin
edible black ink pen

STORING
The finished cake can be kept in a cool, dry place for up to two days.

1 Preheat the oven to 180°C/350°F/ Gas 4. Grease the cake tin, line the base and sides with greaseproof paper and grease the paper. Spoon in the cake mixture and smooth the surface. Bake in the centre of the oven for 35–40 minutes or until a skewer inserted into the centre of the cake comes out clean. Turn out on to a wire rack, peel off the lining paper and leave to cool completely. Trim the top of the cake to make it perfectly flat, then cut horizontally in half.

2 ▲ Spread the chocolate butter icing over one half, then top with the other half. Brush the cake evenly with the apricot jam. Colour about 250 g/ 9 oz of the sugarpaste icing orange. Lightly dust the work surface with icing sugar and roll out the icing until it is large enough to cover the cake. Smooth and ease it over the sides and edges. Trim the edges.

3 ▲ Colour about 50 g/2 oz of the remaining sugarpaste icing green. Colour all but a small ball of the remaining icing purple, then colour the small ball black. Roll out the green and purple icings thinly. Cut the green icing into a rectangle about 1 cm/½ inch smaller than the top surface of the cake. Stick it in place with a little water. Cut the purple icing into a 2.5 x 10 cm/1 x 4 inch strip and stick in place on top of the green rectangle with a little water.

4 Press the sweets for the buttons into one side of the cake through the orange icing, then position the liquorice sweets for the cassette holes, sticking them in place with a little water. Use the edible ink pen to draw tiny lines around the sweets.

5 Cut a few short pieces off the bootlace liquorice and stick on the personal stereo with a little water. Stick the reserved piece of black icing in place at the side of the cake with a little water.

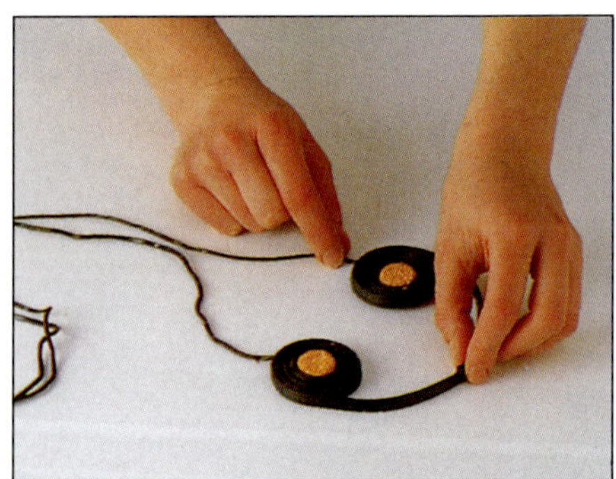

6 ▲ To make the headphones, unravel a little of each of the liquorice wheels and place in position on the table or board, if you are using. Overlap the unravelled ends of the liquorice wheels, sticking them together with a little water. Use a pin or thin metal skewer to make a small hole in the bottoms of the liquorice wheels, then press a liquorice bootlaces into each one. Brush three-quarters of the liquorice bootlace with a little water and stick them together with your fingers, removing the excess water. Press the joined end into the black icing on the cake.

POCKET HARP
MADE IN GERMANY
RT-60MC
MC-60

Basic Cakes

What birthday would be complete without a cake with candles to blow out, or a wedding without a beautifully decorated cake to cut? Some of the most traditional cake recipes provide the best bases for decorating. Recipes for these can be found in this chapter, all of which are used as bases for the decorated cakes found earlier on in the book.

Fruit cake is one of our most popular special occasion cakes. Among its advantages is that it keeps really well, so can be baked well ahead of time and decorated in easy stages. It also provides a wonderfully firm base for all sorts of elegant or novelty decorations. There are other ideas, too, for those who prefer a less rich tasting cake, such as the Madeira or a light fruit cake, as well as a quick-mix sponge for those last-minute, spontaneous celebrations.

Lining Cake Tins

Greaseproof paper is used for lining cake tins. It prevents cakes from sticking to the tin and makes them easier to turn out. Different cake recipes require slightly different techniques of lining, depending on the shape of the tin, the type of cake mixture, and how long the cake needs to cook for.

Lining a shallow round tin
This technique is used for a quick-mix sponge cake.

1 Place the tin on a piece of greaseproof paper and draw around the base of the tin. Cut out the circle just inside the marked line.

2 ▲ Lightly brush the inside of the tin with a vegetable oil and position the paper circle in the base of the tin. Then brush the paper with a little more vegetable oil.

Lining a Swiss roll tin

1 Place the tin on a piece of greaseproof paper and draw around the base. Increase the rectangle by 2.5 cm/1 inch on all sides. Cut out this rectangle and snip each corner diagonally down to the original rectangle.

2 ▲ Lightly brush the inside of the tin with a little vegetable oil and fit the paper into the tin, overlapping the corners slightly so they fit neatly. Brush the paper with a little more vegetable oil.

Lining a deep round cake tin
This technique should be used for all rich or light fruit cakes and Madeira cakes. Use the same method for a square tin, but cut the four sides out separately.

1 Put the tin on a double thickness of greaseproof paper and draw around it. Cut out the circle just inside the line.

2 For the sides of the tin, cut out a double thickness strip of greaseproof paper that will wrap around the outside of the tin, allowing a slight overlap, and which is 2.5 cm/1 inch taller than the depth of the tin.

3 Fold over 2.5 cm/1 inch along the length of the side lining. Snip the paper along its length, inside the fold, at short intervals.

4 Brush the inside of the tin with vegetable oil. Slip the side lining into the tin so the snipped edge fits into the curve of the base and sits flat on the base.

5 ▲ Position the base lining and press it flat. Brush with a little more oil.

Quick-Mix Sponge Cake

Here's a no-fuss, foolproof all-in-one cake, where the ingredients are quickly mixed together. The following quantities and baking instructions are for a deep 20 cm/8 inch sandwich round cake tin or a 20 cm/8 inch ring mould. For other quantities and tin sizes, follow the baking instructions given in the decorated cake recipes.

INGREDIENTS

115 g/4oz/1 cup self-raising flour
1 tsp baking powder
115 g/4 oz/½ cup soft margarine
115 g/4 oz/½ cup caster sugar
2 size 3 eggs

STORING AND FREEZING

The cake can be made up to two days in advance, wrapped in clear film or foil and stored in an airtight container. The cake can be frozen for up to three months.

This is a light quick-mix sponge cake which can be filled and simply decorated with icing for all kinds of special occasions.

FLAVOURINGS

The following amounts are for a single quantity cake. Increase the amounts proportionally for other cake sizes.

Chocolate: Stir 1 tbsp cocoa powder blended with 1 tbsp boiling water into the cake mixture.

Lemon: Stir 2 tsp grated lemon rind into the cake mixture.

1 Preheat the oven to 160°C/325°F/Gas 3. Grease the round cake tin, line the base with greaseproof paper and grease the paper, or grease and flour the ring mould.

2 Sift the flour and baking powder into a bowl. Add the margarine, sugar and eggs.

3 Beat with a wooden spoon for 2–3 minutes. The mixture should be pale in colour and slightly glossy.

4 Spoon the mixture into the prepared tin and smooth the surface. Bake in the centre of the oven for 20–30 minutes. To test if cooked, press the cake lightly in the centre. If firm, the cake is done, if soft, cook for a little longer. Alternatively, insert a skewer into the centre of the cake. If it comes out clean, the cake is ready. Turn out on to a wire rack, remove the lining paper and leave to cool completely.

Truffle Cake Mix

This is a no-cook recipe, using left-over pieces of sponge cake or plain shop-bought sponge to make a moist, rich cake mixture, which is used in several of the children's party cakes.

INGREDIENTS

175 g/6 oz plain sponge cake pieces
175 g/6 oz/2 cups ground almonds
75 g/3oz/scant ½ cup dark brown muscovado sugar
1 tsp ground mixed spice
pinch of ground cinnamon
finely grated zest of 1 orange
3 tbsp freshly squeezed orange juice
5 tbsp clear honey

STORING AND FREEZING

The mixture can be made up to two days in advance, wrapped in clear film and stored in an airtight container. It is not suitable for freezing.

1 Place the sponge cake pieces into the bowl of a food processor or blender and process for a few seconds until they form fine crumbs.

2 Place the cake crumbs, ground almonds, sugar, spices, orange zest, juice and honey in a large mixing bowl. Stir well to combine into a thick, smooth mixture.

3 Use as directed in the children's party cake recipes.

Swiss Roll

Swiss rolls are traditionally made without fat, so they don't keep as long as most other cakes. However, they have a deliciously light texture and provide the cook with the potential for all sorts of luscious fillings and tasty toppings.

INGREDIENTS

4 size 3 eggs, separated
115 g/4 oz/½ cup caster sugar
115 g/4 oz/1 cup plain flour
1 tsp baking powder

STORING AND FREEZING

Swiss rolls and other fat-free sponges do not keep well, so if possible bake on the day you wish to eat it. Otherwise, wrap in clear film or foil and store in an airtight container overnight or freeze for up to three months.

Flavourings

Chocolate: Replace 1½ tbsp flour with 1½ tbsp cocoa powder.

1 Preheat the oven to 180°C/350°F/ Gas 4. Grease a 33 x 23 cm/13 x 19 inch Swiss roll tin, line with greaseproof paper and grease the paper.

2 Whisk the egg whites in a clean, dry bowl until stiff. Beat in 2 tbsp of the caster sugar.

3 Place the egg yolks, remaining caster sugar and 1 tbsp water in a bowl and beat for about 2 minutes until the mixture is pale and leaves a thick trail on the surface when the beaters are lifted up.

4 Sift together the flour and baking powder. Carefully fold the beaten egg yolks into the egg white mixture with a metal spoon. Then carefully fold in the flour mixture.

5 Pour the mixture into the prepared tin and smooth the surface, being careful not to press out any air.

6 Bake in the centre of the oven for 12–15 minutes. To test if cooked, press lightly in the centre. If the cake springs back it is done. It will also start to come away from the edges of the tin.

7 Turn out on to a piece of greaseproof paper lightly sprinkled with caster sugar. Peel off the lining paper and cut off any crisp edges of the cake with a sharp knife. Spread with jam, if wished, and roll up, using the greaseproof paper as a guide. Leave to cool on a wire rack.

Vary the flavour of a traditional Swiss roll by adding a little grated orange, lime or lemon rind to the basic mixture.

Madeira Cake

This fine-textured cake makes a good base for decorating and is therefore a useful alternative to fruit cake, although it will not keep as long. It provides a firmer, longer-lasting base than a Victoria sponge, and can be covered with butter icing, fudge frosting, a thin layer of marzipan or sugarpaste icing. For the ingredients, decide what size and shape of cake you wish to make and then follow the chart on the right.

STORING AND FREEZING
The cake will keep for up to a week, wrapped in clear film or foil and stored in an airtight container. The cake can be frozen for up to three months.

A traditional Madeira cake peaks and cracks slightly on the top. For a flat surface to ice on, simply level off the top with a sharp knife.

Madeira Cake Chart

Cake tin sizes	18 cm/7 in round	20 cm/8 in round	23 cm/9 in round	25 cm/10 in round	30 cm/12 in round
	15 cm/6 in square	18 cm/7 in square	20 cm/8 in square	23 cm/9 in square	28 cm/11 in square
Plain flour	225 g/ 8 oz/ 2 cups	350 g/ 12 oz/ 3 cups	450 g/ 1lb/ 4 cups	500 g/ 1 lb 2 oz/ 4½ cups	625 g/ 1½ lb/ 6 cups
Baking powder	1½ tsp	2 tsp	2½ tsp	1 tbsp	4 tsp
Soft margarine	175 g/ 6 oz/ ¾ cup	250 g/ 9 oz/ 1¼ cups	350 g/ 12 oz/ 1½ cups	400 g/ 14 oz/ 1¾ cups	550 g/ 1 lb 3 oz/ 2¼ cups
Caster sugar	175 g/ 6 oz/ ¾ cup	250 g/ 9 oz/ 1¼ cups	350 g/ 12 oz/ 1½ cups	400 g/ 14 oz/ ¾ cup	500 g/ 1 lb 3 oz/ 2½ cups
Eggs, size 3	3	4	6	7	10
Lemon juice	1 tbsp	1½ tbsp	2 tbsp	2½ tbsp	4 tbsp
Approx. baking time	1¼–1½ hours	1½–1 ¾ hours	1¾–2 hours	1¾–2 hours	2¼–2½ hours

1 Preheat the oven to 160°C/325°F/ Gas 3. Grease a deep cake tin, line the base and sides with a double thickness of greaseproof paper and grease the paper.

2 Sift together the flour and baking powder into a mixing bowl. Add the margarine, sugar, eggs and lemon juice.

3 Stir the ingredients together with a wooden spoon until well combined.

4 Beat the mixture for about 2 minutes until it is glossy.

5 Spoon the mixture into the prepared tin and smooth the top. Bake in the centre of the oven, using the chart above as a guide for timing the size of cake you are baking. If the cake browns too quickly, cover the top loosely with foil. To test if baked, press lightly in the centre. If the cake springs back it is done. Alternatively, insert a skewer into the centre; if it comes out clean the cake is done. Leave the cake to cool in the tin for 5 minutes, then turn out on to a wire rack, remove the lining paper and leave to cool completely.

Rich Fruit Cake

This is the traditional cake mixture for many cakes made for special occasions such as weddings, Christmas, anniversaries and christenings.

Make the cake a few weeks before icing, keep it well wrapped and stored in an airtight container and it should mature beautifully. Because of all its rich ingredients, this fruit cake will keep moist and fresh for several months. Follow the ingredients guide in the chart opposite for the size of cake you wish to make.

1 Preheat the oven to 140°C/275°F/ Gas 1. Grease a deep cake tin, line the base and sides with a double thickness of greaseproof paper and grease the paper.

2 Place the ingredients in a large mixing bowl.

3 Stir to combine, then beat thoroughly with a wooden spoon for 3–6 minutes (depending on size), until well mixed.

4 Spoon the mixture into the prepared tin and smooth the surface with the back of a wet metal spoon. Make a slight impression in the centre to help prevent the cake from doming.

5 Bake in the centre of the oven. Use the chart opposite as a guide for timing the cake you are baking. Test the cake about 30 minutes before the end of the baking time. If the cake browns too quickly, cover the top loosely with foil. To test if baked, press lightly in the centre. If the cake feels firm and when a skewer inserted in the centre comes out clean with no uncooked mixture sticking to it, it is done. Test again at intervals if necessary.

6 Leave the cake to cool in the tin. When completely cool, turn out of the tin. The lining paper can be left on to help keep the cake moist.

STORING AND FREEZING

When the cake is cold, wrap in a double thickness of greaseproof paper or foil. Store in an airtight container in a cool, dry place where it will keep for several months. During storage, the cake can be unwrapped and the bottom brushed with brandy (about half the amount used in the recipe). Re-wrap before storing again. As the cake keeps so well, there is no need to freeze.

A long-lasting cake which is full of rich flavours.

RICH FRUIT CAKE CHART

Cake tin Sizes	15 cm/6 in round 13 cm/5 in square	18 cm/7 in round 15 cm/6 in square	20 cm/8 in round 18 cm/7 in square	23 cm/9 in round 20 cm/8 in square
Currants	200 g/ 7 oz/ 1¼ cups	275 g/ 10 oz/ 1¾ cups	375 g/ 13 oz/ 2¼ cups	450 g/ 1 lb/ 3 cups
Sultanas	115 g/ 4 oz/ ⅔ cup	200 g/ 7 oz/ 1 cup	250 g/ 9 oz/ 1½ cups	300 g/ 11 oz/ 1¾ cups
Raisins	65 g/ 2½ oz/ ⅓ cup	115 g/ 4 oz/ ⅔ cup	150 g/ 5 oz/ ¾ cup	175 g/ 6 oz/ 1 cup
Glacé cherries, halved	40 g/ 1½ oz/ ¼ cup	65 g/ 2½ oz/ ⅓ cup	90 g/ 3½ oz/ ½ cup	115 g/ 4 oz/ ½ cup
Almonds, chopped	40 g/ 1½ oz/ ⅓ cup	65 g/ 2½ oz/ ½ cup	90 g/ 3½ oz/ ¾ cup	115 g/ 4 oz/ 1 cup
Mixed peel	40 g/ 1½ oz/ ¼ cup	65 g/ 2½ oz/ ½ cup	65 g/ 2½ oz/ ½ cup	90 g/ 3½ oz/ ⅔ cup
Lemon, grated rind	½	1	1	2
Brandy	1½ tbsp	2 tbsp	2½ tbsp	3 tbsp
Plain flour	150 g/ 5 oz/ 1⅓ cups	200 g/ 7 oz/ 1¾ cups	250 g/ 9 oz/ 2 cups	300 g/ 11 oz/ 2¾ cups
Ground mixed spice	1 tsp	1 tsp	1¼ tsp	1½ tsp
Ground nutmeg	¼ tsp	½ tsp	½ tsp	1 tsp
Ground almonds	40 g/ 1½ oz/ ½ cup	50 g/ 2 oz/ ⅔ cup	65 g/ 2½ oz/ ¾ cup	75 g/ 3 oz/ 1 cup
Soft margarine or butter	115 g/ 4 oz/ ½ cup	150 g/ 5 oz/ ⅔ cup	200 g/ 7 oz/ ¾ cup	250 g/ 9 oz/ 1¼ cups
Soft brown sugar	130 g 4½ oz/ ⅔ cup	175 g/ 6 oz/ ¾ cup	225 g/ 8 oz/ 1 cup	275 g/ 10 oz/ 1⅓ cups
Black treacle or molasses	1 tbsp	1 tbsp	1 tbsp	1½ tbsp
Eggs, size 3, beaten	3	4	5	6
Approx. baking time	2¼–2½ hours	2½–2¾ hours	3–3½ hours	3¼–3¾ hours

Cake tin sizes	25 cm/10 in round 23 cm/9 in square	28 cm/11 in round 25 cm/10 in square	30 cm/12 in round 28 cm/11 in square	33 cm/13 in round 30 cm/12 in square
Currants	575 g/ 1¼ lb/ 3½ cups	675 g/ 1½ lb/ 4½ cups	800 g/ 1¾ lb/ 5¼ cups	900 g/ 2 lb/ 6 cups
Sultanas	375 g/ 13 oz/ 2 cups	450 g/ 1 lb/ 2½ cups	550 g/ 1 lb 3 oz/ 3 cups	625 g/ 1 lb 6 oz/ 3½ cups
Raisins	200 g/ 7 oz/ 1 cup	225 g/ 8 oz/ 1⅓ cups	250 g/ 9 oz/ 1½ cups	275 g/ 10 oz/ 1½ cups
Glacé cherries, halved	150 g/ 5 oz/ ⅔ cup	175 g/ 6 oz/ ¾ cup	200 g/ 7 oz/ 1 cup	225 g/ 8 oz/ 1¼ cups
Almonds, chopped	150 g 5 oz/ 1¼ cups	175 g/ 6 oz/ 1½ cups	200 g/ 7 oz/ 1⅔ cups	225 g/ 8 oz/ 2 cups
Mixed peel	115 g/ 4 oz/ ¾ cup	150 g/ 5 oz/ 1 cup	175 g/ 6 oz/ 1 cup	200 g/ 7 oz/ 1⅓ cups
Lemon, grated rind	2	2	3	3
Brandy	3½ tbsp	4 tbsp	4½ tbsp	5 tbsp
Plain flour	400 g/ 14 oz/ 3½ cups	450 g/ 1 lb/ 4 cups	550 g/ 1 lb 3 oz/ 4½ cups	625 g/ 1 lb 6 oz/ 5½ cups
Ground mixed spice	1½ tsp	2 tsp	2½ tsp	1 tbsp
Ground nutmeg	1 tsp	1 tsp	1½ tsp	2 tsp
Ground almonds	90 g/ 3½ oz/ 1¼ cups	115 g/ 4 oz/ 1⅓ cups	130 g/ 4½ oz/ 1½ cups	150 g/ 5 oz/ 1⅔ cups
Soft margarine or butter	300 g/ 11 oz/ scant 1½ cups	375 g/ 13 oz/ scant 1¾ cups	425 g/ 15 oz/ scant 2 cups	500 g/ 1 lb 2 oz/ 2¼ cups
Soft brown sugar	350 g/ 12 oz 1½ cups	400 g/ 14 oz/ scant 2 cups	450 g/ 1 lb/ 2 cups	475 g/ 1 lb 2 oz/ 2¼ cups
Black treacle or molasses	2 tbsp	2 tbsp	2 tbsp	2½ tbsp
Eggs, beaten	7	8	9	10
Approx. baking time	3¾–4¼ hours	4–4½ hours	4½–5¼ hours	5¼–5¾ hours

Light Fruit Cake

For those who prefer a lighter, less dense fruit cake, here is a less rich version, still ideal for marzipanning and covering with sugarpaste or royal icing. Follow the ingredients guide in the chart on the right according to the size of cake you wish to make.

STORING AND FREEZING
When the cake is cold, wrap well in greaseproof paper, clear film or foil. If stored in an airtight container it will keep for several weeks. As the cake keeps so well, you do not usually need to freeze it. However, you could freeze it for up to three months.

1 Preheat the oven to 150°C/300°F/ Gas 2. Grease a deep cake tin, line the base and sides with a double thickness of greaseproof paper and grease the paper.

2 Place all the ingredients together in a large mixing bowl.

3 Stir to combine, then beat thoroughly with a wooden spoon for 3–4 minutes, depending on the size, until well mixed.

4 Spoon the mixture into the prepared tin and smooth the surface with the back of a wet metal spoon. Make a slight impression in the centre to help prevent the cake from doming.

5 Bake in the centre of the oven. Use the chart on the right as a guide for timing the size of cake you are baking. Test the cake about 15 minutes before the end of the baking time. If the cake browns too quickly, cover the top loosely with foil. To test if baked, press lightly in the centre. If the cake feels firm, and when a skewer inserted in the centre comes out clean with no uncooked mixture sticking to it, it is done. Test again at intervals if necessary.

6 Leave the cake to cool in the tin. When completely cool, turn out of the tin. The lining paper can be left on to help keep the cake moist.

Round, square, ring or heart-shaped - the shape of this light fruit cake can be varied to suit the occasion.

LIGHT FRUIT CAKE CHART

Cake tin sizes	15 cm/6 in round 13 cm/5 in square	18 cm/7 in round 15 cm/6 in square	20 cm/8 in round 18 cm/7 in square	23 cm/9 in round 20 cm/8 in square
Soft margarine or butter	115 g/ 4 oz/ ½ cup	175 g/ 6 oz/ ¾ cup	225 g/ 8 oz/ 1 cup	275 g/ 10 oz/ 1⅓ cups
Caster sugar	115 g/ 4 oz/ ½ cup	175 g/ 6 oz/ ¾ cup	225 g/ 8 oz/ 1 cup	275 g/ 10 oz/ 1⅓ cups
Orange, grated rind	½	½	1	1
Eggs, size 3, beaten	3	4	5	6
Plain flour	165 g 5½ oz/ 1½ cups	200 g/ 7 oz/ 1¾ cups	300 g/ 11 oz/ 2¾ cups	400 g/ 14 oz/ 3½ cups
Baking powder	¼ tsp	½ tsp	½ tsp	1 tsp
Ground mixed spice	1 tsp	1½ tsp	2 tsp	2½ tsp
Currants	50 g/ 2 oz/ ⅓ cup	115 g/ 4 oz/ ⅔ cup	175 g/ 6 oz/ 1 cup	225 g/ 8 oz/ 1½ cups
Sultanas	50 g/ 2 oz/ ⅓ cup	115 g/ 4 oz/ ⅔ cup	175 g/ 6 oz/ 1 cup	225 g/ 8 oz/ 1⅓ cups
Raisins	50 g/ 2 oz/ ⅓ cup	115 g/ 4 oz/ ⅔ cup	175 g/ 6 oz/ 1 cup	225 g/ 8 oz/ 1⅓ cups
Dried apricots, chopped	25 g/ 1 oz/ 7–8	50 g/ 2 oz/ 14	50 g/ 2 oz/ 14	75 g/ 3 oz/ 21
Mixed cut peel	50 g/ 2 oz/ scant ½ cup	75 g/ 3 oz/ good ½ cup	115 g/ 4 oz/ ¾ cup	150 g/ 5 oz/ 1 cup
Approx. baking time	2¼–2½ hours	2½–2¾ hours	2¾–3¼ hours	3¼–3¾ hours

Basic Icings

Cakes can take on many guises, and nothing enhances their appearance more for that extra special occasion than a little icing. This chapter offers a range of simple classic icing recipes to suit the type of cake you have made and which can be adapted according to the occasion. Ideas range from quick-mix icings that may be instantly poured, spread, swirled or piped on to sponge and Madeira cakes or Swiss rolls, to the more regal icings, such as royal icing and sugarpaste icing. These are ideal for decorating fruit cakes for more formal occasions, like anniversaries, christenings and weddings.

The icings in this section are all fairly traditional, and can be used with imagination to create special effects on cakes. If you want to substitute any of them with a favourite icing recipe, make sure it suits the cake you are working on.

Glacé Icing

This icing can be made in just a few minutes and can be varied by adding a little food colouring or flavouring. The following quantity makes enough to cover the top and decorate a 20 cm/8 inch round sponge cake.

Ingredients

Makes 225 g/8 oz

225 g/8 oz/2 cups icing sugar
2-3 tbsp warm water or fruit juice
food colouring (optional)

STORING

This icing should be used straight away.

1 Sift the icing sugar into a bowl. Using a wooden spoon, gradually stir in enough water to make an icing that is the consistency of thick cream. Beat until the icing is smooth. It should be thick enough to coat the back of the spoon. If it is too runny, beat in a little more sifted icing sugar.

2 To colour the icing, beat in a few drops of food colouring. Use the icing immediately for coating or piping.

Drizzled or spread, glacé icing can quickly turn a plain cake into something special.

Marzipan

With its smooth, pliable texture, marzipan has been a popular icing for centuries in cake making, especially for large cakes like wedding and christening cakes. It is also excellent for making a variety of cake decorations. Marzipan is applied to the sides and top of a cake, particularly rich fruit cakes, to prevent moisture seeping through the cake and to provide a smooth undercoat for the top covering of royal or sugarpaste icing. Once the marzipan has been applied, leave it to dry for at least 12 hours before applying the icing. For a richer taste you can mix up your own marzipan . However, if you have any concerns about using raw eggs in uncooked recipes, especially in light of current health warnings, do buy ready-made marzipan. It is very good quality and does not contain raw egg and is available in two colours, white and yellow. White is the best choice if you want to add your own colours and create different moulded shapes.

The following recipe is sufficient to cover the top and sides of an 18 cm/ 7 inch round or a 15 cm/6 inch square cake. Make half the amount if only the top is to be covered.

INGREDIENTS

Makes 450 g/1 lb

225 g/8 oz/2¼ cups ground almonds
115 g/4 oz/1 cup icing sugar, sifted
115 g/4 oz/½ cup caster sugar
1 tsp lemon juice
2 drops almond essence
1 size 4 egg, beaten

STORING

The marzipan will keep for up to four days, in a sealed airtight container and stored in a fridge.

1 Put the ground almonds, icing and caster sugars into a bowl and mix together.

2 Add the lemon juice, almond essence and enough beaten egg to mix to a soft but firm dough. Gather it together with your fingers to form a ball.

3 Knead the marzipan on a work surface lightly dusted with sifted icing sugar until smooth.

Marzipan can be used as an attractive cake coating in its own right as well as providing a base for other icings.

Sugarpaste Icing

Sugarpaste icing has opened up a whole new concept in cake decorating. It is wonderfully pliable, easy to make and use, and can be coloured, moulded and shaped in the most imaginative fashion. Though quick to make at home, shop-bought sugarpaste, also known as easy-roll or ready-to-roll icing, is very good quality and handy to use. Ready-made sugarpaste does not contain raw egg, so do use if you have any concerns about uncooked egg in the light of current health warnings.

This recipe makes sufficient to cover the top and sides of an 18 cm/7 inch round or a 15 cm/6 inch square cake.

Sugarpaste icing can be moulded to make decorations to suit any cake.

INGREDIENTS

Makes 350 g/12 oz

1 size 3 egg white

1 tbsp liquid glucose, warmed

350 g/12 oz/3 cups icing sugar, sifted

STORING

The icing will keep for up to one week, wrapped in clear film or a plastic bag and stored in a fridge. Bring to room temperature before use. If a thin crust forms, trim off before using or it will make the icing lumpy. Also, if the icing dries out or hardens, knead in a little boiled water to make it smooth and pliable again.

1 Put the egg white and glucose in a mixing bowl. Stir them together to break up the egg white.

2 Add the icing sugar and mix together with a palette knife or knife, using a chopping action, until well blended and the icing begins to bind together.

3 Knead the mixture with your fingers until it forms a ball.

4 Knead the sugarpaste on a work surface lightly dusted with icing sugar for several minutes until smooth, soft and pliable. If the icing is too soft, knead in some more sifted icing sugar until it is firm and pliable.

Royal Icing

Royal icing has gained a regal position in the world of icing. Any special occasion cake that demands a classical, professional finish uses this smooth icing. If you are concerned about current health warnings advising against the use of raw eggs in uncooked recipes then buy ready-made royal icing.

This recipe makes sufficient icing to cover the top and sides of an 18 cm/7 inch round or a 15 cm/6 inch square cake. Even when working with royal icing, always keep it covered.

Ingredients

Makes 675 g/1½ lb

3 size 3 egg whites
about 675 g/1½ lb/6 cups icing sugar, sifted
1½ tsp glycerine
few drops lemon juice
colouring (optional)

A classic look for a classic royal icing.

STORING

Royal icing will keep for up to three days, stored in a plastic container with a tight fitting lid in a fridge.

1 Put the egg whites in a bowl and stir lightly to break them up.

2 Add the icing sugar gradually, beating well with a wooden spoon, between each addition. Add sufficient icing sugar to make a smooth, shiny icing that is the consistency of very stiff meringue. It should be thin enough to spread, but thick enough to hold its shape when spread.

3 Beat in the glycerine, lemon juice and food colouring, if using.

4 It is best to let the icing sit for about 1 hour before using. Cover with a piece of damp clear film or a lid. Before using, stir the icing to burst any air bubbles.

Icing Consistencies

For flat icing

The recipe to the left is for a consistency of icing suitable for flat icing a rich fruit cake covered in marzipan. When the spoon is lifted out of the icing, it should form a sharp point, with a slight curve at the end, known as 'soft peak'.

For piping

For piping purposes, the icing needs to be slightly stiffer than for peaked icing so that it forms a fine sharp peak when the spoon is lifted out. This allows the icing to flow easily for piping, at the same time enabling it to keep its definition.

The right consistency

To stiffen icing, add a little sifted icing sugar or to make it thinner beat in a little egg white. Do this carefully as a little of one or the other will change the consistency fairly quickly.

Butter Icing

The creamy rich flavour and silky smoothness of butter icing is popular with both children and adults. It can be varied in colour and flavour and makes a decorative filling and coating for sponge and Madeira cakes or Swiss rolls. Simply swirled, or more elaborately piped, butter icing gives a delicious and attractive finish.

The following recipe makes enough to fill and coat the sides and top of a 20 cm/8 inch sponge cake.

Ingredients

Makes 350 g/12 oz

75 g/3 oz/6 tbsp soft margarine or butter, softened
225 g/8 oz/2 cups icing sugar, sifted
1 tsp vanilla essence
2-3 tsp milk

STORING

The icing will keep for up to three days, in an airtight container stored in a fridge.

1 Put the margarine or butter, icing sugar, vanilla essence and 1 tsp of the milk in a bowl.

2 Beat with a wooden spoon or an electric mixer, adding sufficient extra milk to give a light, smooth and fluffy consistency.

Flavourings

Chocolate: Blend 1 tbsp cocoa powder with 1 tbsp hot water. Omit the milk. Allow to cool before beating into the icing.
Coffee: Blend 2 tsp instant coffee powder or granules with 1 tbsp boiling water. Allow to cool before beating into the icing. Omit the milk.
Lemon, orange or lime: Substitute the vanilla essence and milk for lemon, orange or lime juice and 2 tsp of finely grated citrus zest. Omit the zest if using the icing for piping. Lightly colour the icing with the appropriate shade of food colouring, if wished.

Generous swirls of butter icing give a mouth-watering effect to a cake.

Fudge Frosting

A rich, darkly delicious frosting, this can transform a simple sponge cake into one worthy of a very special occasion. Spread fudge frosting smoothly over the cake or swirl it. Or be even more elaborate with a little piping – it really is very versatile. The following amount will fill and coat the top and sides of a 20 cm/8 inch or 23 cm/9 inch round sponge cake.

INGREDIENTS
Makes 350 g/12 oz
50 g/2 oz/2 squares plain chocolate
225 g/8 oz/1½ cups icing sugar, sifted
50 g/2 oz/4 tbsp butter or margarine
3 tbsp milk or single cream
1 tsp vanilla essence

1 Break or chop the chocolate into small pieces. Put the chocolate, icing sugar, butter, milk and vanilla essence in a heavy-based saucepan.

2 Stir over a very low heat until the chocolate and butter melt. Remove from the heat and stir until evenly blended.

3 Beat the icing frequently as it cools until it thickens sufficiently to use for spreading or piping. Use immediately and work quickly once it has reached the right consistency.

STORING
This icing should be used straight away.

Thick glossy swirls of fudge icing are almost a decoration in themselves.

Piping Bags

Piping bags are available ready-made in a washable fabric. Icing syringes are also good for the beginner to learn on, and are useful for piping butter icing in bold designs. However, for more intricate piping, particularly if using a variety of icing colours and nozzles, home-made piping bags from greaseproof paper are more practical and more flexible to handle. Make up several ahead of time, then fit them with straight-sided nozzles. Do not use nozzles with ridges, as they do not have such a tight fit in the bag. To prevent the icing drying out, cover the nozzle ends with a damp cloth when not in use.

1 ▲ Cut out a 25 cm/10 in square of greaseproof paper. Fold it in half diagonally to make a triangle.

2 ▲ Hold the paper, with the point of the triangle facing you and with your thumb in the middle of the longest edge.

3 ▲ Hold the left corner and bring it over to meet the point of the triangle

4 ▲ Hold in position and bring the remaining corner round and back over to meet the other two points, to form a cone shape. Holding all the points together, position them to make sure the cone is tight and the point of it is sharp. With the cone open, turn the points neatly inside the top edge, creasing firmly. Secure with a staple.

5 For using with a nozzle, cut a small straight piece off the pointed end of the bag and position the nozzle so it fits snugly into the point. To use without a nozzle, fill the bag two-thirds full with icing and cut a small straight piece off the end to pipe lines.

6 For ease and control, it is important to hold the bag in a relaxed position. You may find it easier to hold it with one or both hands. For one hand, hold the bag between your middle and index fingers and push out the icing with your thumb. If using both hands, simply wrap the other hand around the bag in the same manner, so both thumbs can push the icing out.

7 ▲ To pipe, hold the bag so the nozzle is directly over the area you want to pipe on. The bag will be held straight or at an angle, depending on the shape you are piping. To release the icing, gently press down on the top of the bag. and lift your thumb to stop the flow of icing. Use a palette knife to cut off any excess icing from the tip of the nozzle as you lift the bag from each piped shape, to keep the shapes neat.

Food Colourings

Food colourings and tints for cake making are available today in almost as large a range as those found on an artist's palette. This has opened up endless possibilities for the cake decorator to create the most imaginative and colourful designs.

Liquid colours are suitable for marzipan, butter icing and sugarpaste icing when only a few drops are required to tint the icing. If used in large amounts, they will soften the icings too much. So for vibrant, stronger colours, as well as for subtle sparkling tints, use pastes or powders, available from cake icing specialists. These are so concentrated you only need a little to create the most vivid effects, and they will not change the consistency of the icing. Food colouring pens, available in colours such as candy pink, blueberry blue and spice brown, can be used to add fine details to cakes, or to create a whole picture. When choosing colours for icings, ensure they are harmonious, and that they complement your design.

To Colour Icings

Colour is added differently, depending on whether it is in liquid form, a paste or powder. While working with the colourings, it is best to stand them on a plate or washable board so they do not mark your work surface. Use cocktail sticks for transferring the colour to the icing, using a clean one for each colour so the colours do not become mixed.

Liquid Colour

This can be added a few drops at a time until the required shade is reached, and stirred into softer icings, such as butter, royal or glacé.

Paste Colour

1 Colour has to be kneaded into firmer icings, such as sugarpaste and marzipan. Dip a cocktail stick into the colouring and streak it on to the surface of a ball of the icing.

2 Knead thoroughly until it is evenly worked in and there is no streaking. Add sparingly at first, remembering that the colour becomes more intense as the icing stands, then leave for about 10 minutes to see if is the shade you need.

Powder Colour

To create subtle tintings in specific areas, brush powdered colourings on to the surface of the icing.